HARDPRESS .NET

ISBN: 9781313377706

Published by:
HardPress Publishing
8345 NW 66TH ST #2561
MIAMI FL 33166-2626

Email: info@hardpress.net
Web: http://www.hardpress.net

HOW TO LOOK AT PICTURES

HOW TO LOOK AT PICTURES

BY

ROBERT CLERMONT WITT, B.A.

LONDON

GEORGE BELL AND SONS

1902

A. 162058

CHISWICK PRESS : CHARLES WHITTINGHAM AND CO.
TOOKS COURT, CHANCERY LANE, LONDON.

TO

M. H. W.

PREFACE

THIS little book makes no attempt to be original. It is intended for those who have no special knowledge of pictures and painting, but are interested in them, and find themselves from time to time in public and private galleries and exhibitions. It will, therefore, make no appeal to the artist, the expert or the professional critic. Much art-criticism at the present day is so deeply erudite, or so special and scientific, that its influence is necessarily limited to those among the initiated who, after years of study and probation, can enter fully into its mysteries, and are therefore in no need of such simple suggestions as are offered here.

In case it should be objected by readers of more exquisite sensibilities that in these pages the emotions excited by the beauty of pictorial art are ignored, or treated in too homely and matter-of-fact a manner, I would suggest that these more subtle and fleeting impressions of beauty, these aromas from another world, do not require to be called forth by words, but come unbidden in the fulness of time to every lover of pictures. Moreover, recognising their pure essence and perfect delicacy, I have feared to mar by description that which no words can adequately render.

HEVER,
KENT,
1902.

CONTENTS

LIST OF ILLUSTRATIONS

INTRODUCTION

AMONG the most pathetic figures in the world must be counted the men and women·who may be seen in any picture-gallery slowly circumambulating the four walls with eyes fixed upon catalogue or guide-book, only looking up at intervals to insure that they are standing before the right picture. All unknowing they falter on, achieving only fatigue of body and mind, with a certain mournful satisfaction in a toilsome task nearing accomplishment. Again and again they find themselves looking at famous pictures without seeing them. They are conscious that some wonderful power lies hidden there, but they do not know the charmed word to release it. They feel sure they should be interested ; at the same time they know they are bored. Whatever appreciation they have is too capricious, too purely personal to claim their confidence in its justice or intelligence. Its principles cannot bear analysis, and are rudely shaken under cross-examination. They do indeed deeply honour the names of the great masters upon the picture-frames ; some slight acquaintance with them inspires reverence and respect, but where it goes beyond this it is for the most part undiscriminating and unreasoning hero-worship. The catalogue is of little use from this point of view. It merely gives the name and date of the artist and possibly his school, or, if more ambitious in its construction, some account of his life, with a bald, prosaic description of the picture, a description which only emphasises the absence of what the weary seeker after enjoyment hopes to find ready to his hand.

We long to feel at home in a collection of pictures, instead of lost in a strange world and out of touch with its inhabitants. Not a city of importance in Europe but has acquired or is acquiring its picture-gallery. Not a house or cottage but contains some form of pictorial art. Yet there is little or no literature dealing with pictures from the point of view of how to look at them. Elaborate monographs of artists, philosophies of art, treatises on aesthetics, exhaustive disquisitions on the various schools of painting—all these exist in overwhelming abundance. But they demand years of patient study. And indeed there is no book written, or ever to be written, which will suddenly transform the industrious and well-intentioned reader into the just and experienced critic. The art of seeing pictures is not contained in rules or formulae. Books alone can no more teach how to see pictures than how to paint them. And another and most powerful deterrent to the careful consideration of pictures is undoubtedly their vast multitude. The number of works of the first order alone is indeed almost discouraging. A great gallery contains, perhaps, some thousands of pictures, of which many hundreds are of real merit. The difficulty of concentrating the attention on any particular picture is one which even experienced critics feel keenly, especially in a gallery where all is new and strange. The eye wanders from the picture on which it should be fixed to that which hangs close by, above or below. Unfortunately exigencies of space and expense render the proper hanging of pictures almost impossible. There are few collections so well hung as that in Trafalgar Square, and yet even there the frames jostle one another so closely that the eye tends to pass on, leaving the mind, as it were, a picture or two behind. There is no doubt that the enjoyment of even an inferior picture hanging alone or in scant company in the house of a friend is relatively greater than that of a collection of masterpieces crowded together in a great gallery.

There are other difficulties arising from the actual arrangement of pictures, especially in the great public collections. The plan favoured in the more conservative galleries of hanging together in one central room a number of the most celebrated pictures without consideration of the schools to which they belong, a plan adopted in the Salon Carré of the Louvre, the Tribuna in the Uffizi and the Sala de la Reina Isabel in the Prado, has many objections. In such a " Holy of Holies " the opportunity of comparison with lesser works by the same artists, or with the best works of lesser artists, is lost, and the masterpieces tend to suffer from their very uniformity of excellence. Again, the pictures are thus, as it were, taken out of their context. An excellent example of the practical working of this system with its obvious drawbacks may be seen in the Louvre. Formerly Van Eyck's small, gem-like *Madonna with the Chancellor Rollin* used to hang inconspicuous and lost among the larger masterpieces of other schools in the Salon Carré. It has lately been removed to a small cabinet devoted to works of the early Flemish school, where this marvellous example of minute and delicate painting asserts its undoubted supremacy among its compatriots, hanging as the centre of attraction and in the place of honour. On the other hand, we have lost the opportunity of comparing one of the finest masterpieces of early Flemish painting with works occupying a like position in other schools. The more modern system, followed in the galleries of London and Berlin, and most of the great European collections, of arranging the pictures according to their schools, and as far as possible in some chronological order, offers obvious advantages to the student. The rise and fall of schools, the gradual evolution of individual genius, the connection between master and pupil, may thus be easily traced.

It must also be remembered that a spacious well-lighted gallery is not always the best setting for every picture. Old pictures were not painted with an eye to the uniform requirements of the modern picture-gallery, where individual wants cannot possibly be considered. Many were intended to serve as altar-pieces in the dim religious light of church or cathedral, often indeed designed to fit into the architectural framework of the altar. In some cases where the painter has consciously adapted his picture to such a position, much of its effect is lost in the cruel glare of a picture-gallery. Even so magnificent a work as Titian's *Assumption* appears comparatively hard and crude in colour in its new home in the Academy at Venice, though over the high altar of the Frari Church, for which it was painted, the bright blues, reds and yellows would have been mellowed and subdued. Again, until but the other day how lost and purposeless appeared the vast series of canvases designed by Rubens for Marie de Medicis for the decoration of the Luxembourg, skied and scattered as they were about the long corridor in the Louvre, failing to dominate yet contriving to kill the surrounding crowd of smaller pictures. Now, however, framed into the very walls of the spacious Salle Rubens, specially designed for their sole reception, they may be appreciated at their true value as one magnificent and consistent scheme of pictorial decoration rather than as a number of isolated units.

Many pictures, notably those of the Dutch School, on the other hand, were painted to hang in the limited space and moderate light of a dwelling-room. These are lost on the large wall expanse of a high gallery lighted from the top. To them the system now being introduced wherever possible of small cabinets lighted by side windows instead of from the ceiling is admirably suited, care being taken that the light on the picture is adequate and falls from the side intended by the painter.

These are among the more obvious and practical difficulties which meet us at the outset, and bear only indirectly on the study of pictures. There are many other points of view to consider in looking at pictures, which need only to be suggested to appeal at once to the spectator. They in their turn suggest others. The standpoint widens, and the spirit of criticism is awakened. Pictures which before

we have passed
Perhaps a hundred times, nor cared to see,

acquire an interest, a fascination for us that is in the nature of a revelation. Our purely intellectual pleasure in the puzzles and problems of pictorial art, its historical and archaeological sides, grows to be of the keenest. Wholly distinct from these our aesthetic delight in the beauties of form and colour increases with each new discovery. Enjoyment follows hard upon understanding. Every branch of the graphic arts gains a special and peculiar interest. A collection becomes the meeting-place of familiar friends and faces. With experience and knowledge, each picture falls into its place in the mind, is associated with others, suggests comparisons and parallels and a sense of the essential unity of pictorial art. A feeling of mastery over a whole world of beautiful forms and colours takes the place of impotent and vexa-

tious uncertainty.   True, there are many pretty quarrels
to be picked.   The critic who could say " I bite my
thumb at no man " is not easy to find, and when discovered he would no doubt prove to be unworthy the
title.   But the controversial side of art-criticism, though
it has a peculiar fascination of its own, would be out of
place in these pages, which are intended to offer suggestions rather than to make converts.

There is no last word in art-criticism, or if there be it
remains unspoken.   It is impossible to work out any
complete theory which will answer all questions and solve
all difficulties.   Many of the problems that inevitably
arise must rest unsolved, the questions admitting of too
many different answers.   It is merely proposed here to
set down some of the points of view which naturally
occur to the spectator who stands before a picture.   No
attempt will be made to decide for the reader what
pictures should or should not be especially admired, but
rather to enable him to *see* pictures in the fullest sense
of the word, to understand and appreciate them, and to
decide for himself what are the worthiest objects of his
admiration.   For it is the whole-hearted enjoyment which
comes with growing powers of appreciation that gives
painting, and indeed all art, its fascination for most of
us.   Sympathy and whatever of the artist there may be
in each of us enables us to read something of our own
into the most perfect picture ever painted, something of
which even the painter never dreamed.   Painting is no
dry-as-dust subject, a thing of museums, of value only
when carefully catalogued and classified, and to be studied
by the industrious apprentice with an eye to prospective
advancement.   Art is no substitute for science, but
rather the adornment of life, completing what without it
were but imperfect.

HOW TO LOOK AT PICTURES

CHAPTER I

THE PERSONAL POINT OF VIEW

THE personal point of view is naturally the first to be touched upon. Criticism is as personal and as various as the art of painting itself. In looking at a picture the spectator's own temperament and ideals, his education and experience will more than any other factors influence his attitude towards it. And as these vary indefinitely with every individual, it is vain to attempt to analyse them at length. There are, however, some general considerations of interest.

The spectator may be either an artist by training and profession, or a layman with no special knowledge of the art of painting. Their points of view will almost necessarily differ. Artist and layman see with other eyes. They look for other things. The artist, in the full consciousness of his greater experience in matters artistic, is convinced of the essential superiority of the spirit and letter of his criticism over the superficial reasoning of the amateur. The layman quotes the ancient proverb that onlookers see most of the game, and thanks God that he at least is not prejudiced in favour of any one narrow school or clique even as this artist. The antagonism is as old as art itself. Speaking generally, the layman is in

B

the right.   Disraeli's witticism that the critics are those
who have failed in literature or art contains but a grain
of truth.   The best art-critics certainly have not been
artists.   Ruskin, indeed, might have been either, but his
case is somewhat exceptional.   Onlookers do indeed see
most of the game ; but only if they know the rules.   The
great art-critic is as sadly to seek as the great artist, and
is almost as complex a being.   He is born, not made.
Even his birthright, however, will not suffice without
wide and careful study.   He must combine keen powers
of observation, judgment and discrimination with something of the sacred flame and inspired enthusiasm of the
artist.

But, short of this, there is a sense in which we are all
critics, in that we deliberately take upon ourselves to
pass in judgment the pictures which hang before us.
The point of view which generally first finds expression
is that of personal like or dislike, love or hate.   It is
indeed the most rudimentary form of criticism, and yet
it contains something of the stuff of which criticism is
made.   Representing as it usually does an unreasoned
and unintelligent personal prejudice in favour of any
particular picture or school, it is valueless.   Based on
the other hand on experience, observation, careful comparison and study, it becomes the last word of art-
criticism.   Praise or blame should, therefore, be not the
first but the last point of view from which to regard
pictures.   The desire to understand should precede the
wish to extol or condemn.   Full understanding should
in its attitude be appreciative rather than condemnatory.
Tout comprendre est tout pardonner applies in art as in
morals, and although this habit of mind can be exaggerated, may even lead to that "indifferent and tepid appreciation of all and sundry, especially if consecrated by

age," which in the end is destructive of the best interests
of art, the general tendency, at least among beginners, is
to err on the side of extreme severity and wholesale
condemnation.   It is far easier to observe faults than
to recognise excellences.   It is not always easy to remember that even if the picture as a whole fails to
please, it may contain charming passages of colour or
subtleties of drawing which render it worthy of attention.   On the other hand, the first impression of a seem-
ingly attractive *ensemble* may prove unable to bear closer
analysis.   We do not, indeed, feel in sympathy with
every picture or even with every school of painting.
The personal equation is too strong for that.   But we
can at least appreciate admirable qualities, whether in
technique or style, wherever they exist.   Some pictures
there are to which, like certain books, we feel always
drawn, in whose presence we enjoy a peculiar sense of
intimacy and well-being.   With these we like to live.
Such inclinations are purely individual.   Other pictures
again, less intimate friends, are reserved for occasional
intercourse, being less well adapted for our daily wants.
But no such personal considerations can affect the question of the real value of a picture, though the test is too
often applied.

There are many to be found, especially among those
whose want of knowledge and experience is their sole
qualification to the title of unprejudiced critics, who
profess to have so high a standard that they will only
look at the few great masterpieces in each collection,
and entirely refuse to consider any picture falling short
of these.   " Nothing is so painful to me," said Sainte-
Beuve, " as to see the disdain with which people often
treat commendable and distinguished writers of the
second order as if there were no room save for those of

the first." And the protest is equally applicable to art. But if an attitude of undue severity is narrowing, the blind and bigoted admiration of any one master or school is equally fatal. The great artist is indeed often a man of one idea, and that very fact the secret of his greatness. But this is a peculiarity of the creative mind, and where admiration is exaggerated and unbalanced in the critic and excludes all other aspects of art, it can only stultify, not strengthen. The critic of but one idea is indeed poorly endowed for his vocation. Excellence in painting as in all else is comparative. A moderate picture hanging in a collection of vastly inferior works often surprises and delights the eye, while if placed among first-rate pictures it finds its true level. Yet even a fifth-rate picture has always some one or more redeeming quality to the trained and practised eye. There is scarcely a painting in any great collection, especially in one so carefully chosen as our National Gallery, which will not amply repay careful study.

Granting, then, that criticism must from its very nature be personal, the question arises as to its value. The much abused " It is a matter of Taste" expresses the difficulty in its most popular form. This is not the place to discuss the vexed question of authority in matters of art. But a real difficulty undoubtedly exists in the minds of many who have discussed and disputed the merits of this or that work of art. Is A's opinion as valuable as B's? By what right does C profess to judge between them? And to whom does the ultimate appeal lie? The difficulty is one which must be faced. If my personal opinion as to the merits of any given picture is as valuable as that of my neighbour, independently of whether either has studied painting in all or any of its branches, then indeed there is no disputing about matters

of taste.   The absurdity of this position is self-evident.
Again, it may happen that we have each of us devoted
a long lifetime to the consideration and observation of
pictures and yet differ widely in our estimate.   Time
alone can decide.   " The greatest art," says Symonds,
" communicates the greatest amount of satisfaction to
the greatest number of normal human beings throughout
the greatest length of time."   And as a rough working
hypothesis this may serve our purpose, though it is far
from proving a principle of uniform and universal
application.

The period of probation can indeed be no short one,
for the disturbing and strange vagaries of fashion are
overpoweringly strong.   One generation applauds what
its successor despises.   The heroes of the present are
disregarded when their vogue is past.   Our verdict upon
our contemporaries may be reversed by those who come
after us.   Our grandfathers admired the Italian painters
of the seventeenth century, Guido and the Carracci, and
cared nothing for the Primitives.   We have reversed this
estimate, and the auction-room is the barometer which
records these changes of fashion.   Phases and vogues of
this kind there must always be in which even the leaders
of opinion will seem unanimous for the moment.   All
these come to the test of time.   Slowly but surely the
artist finds his rightful place in the long roll of names.
The exaggerations and enthusiasms of each generation
fall into their true perspective.   The dominating personalities of our own country, our own day, take quite other
proportions when ranged alongside of the giants of
other countries, other centuries.   The most irreconcilable
views resolve themselves into something like general
unanimity.   Old disputes and antagonisms tend to
become buried in their own dust.   And this growing

consensus of opinion applies not only to the greatest masters but to the long list of names which rank after them.

Unanimity indeed is impossible, and our working hypothesis, if too closely pressed, shows signs of giving out. The truth is that, broadly speaking and subject to the insensate changes of fashion, time does afford the surest test of real merit. It is now universally admitted that such men as Leonardo, Raphael, Michelangelo, Titian, Rubens, Rembrandt, Velasquez and Turner were artists of the most splendid genius; that others like Perugino, Luini, Memlinc, Teniers, Murillo and Hogarth were painters of great power but of less extraordinary attainments. It is only when we come to estimate the comparative position of the individuals among their peers that critics equally qualified to judge will be found in hopeless disagreement. And this must always be; the personal element plays so considerable a part with each of us. The enthusiast of realism will prize Velasquez before Raphael. Those who care above all for magnificent colour and exuberant vitality admire Rubens more than Leonardo. To Titian we go for grandeur and stately tranquillity, to Rembrandt for mystery and character, to Turner for imaginative vision, and according as we set store by these qualities we rank their exponents in our Calendar.

Further, our own personal likings change with age and increased experience. The idols of childhood and youth have often fallen before middle age. This is due, no doubt, to some extent to the growth of our powers of criticism, but it is also largely temperamental and independent of the intellect. Fortunately the thought that our judgment of our immediate predecessors and contemporaries is by no means infallible need not discourage. On the contrary, the need for careful judgment is the more imperative. On the opinions of the past and the present the verdict of the future will be founded. The unknown artist of to-day may come to be one of the greatest names. The idea adds dignity to the task of judging our contemporaries. There is the more need of bold and independent criticism which, without arrogating to itself any finality, is prepared to stand by and justify its judgments. Only with experience can the confidence that comes of the sense of power and mastery over the subject be attained. Courage in criticism is as valuable as in art itself. There is no antagonism between this courage and the authority which time and study have sanctioned. Authority in contemporary art is based on study of the art which has gone before as well as on that of the present. For the wholly unstudied critic of modern painting to set up his horn against the trained and experienced student is presumption, not courage. But among those who have qualified themselves to judge of pictures on which time has not yet pronounced a final verdict, there is room for the most fearless criticism. " To know what you prefer," said R. L. Stevenson, " instead of humbly saying 'Amen' to what the world tells you you ought to prefer, is to have kept your soul alive." Honesty in criticism is terrified by the bogey of Authority. But authority, with her exclusive list of great names, is only terrible to those who do not look into her title to the claim. We read that a certain well-known art-critic has declared that some one contemporary artist is the greatest master of portraiture or landscape, of animal painting or still life, the world has ever seen, or that the canvases of another are unworthy of even the most passing attention. If we know nothing of pictures or painting, we are fain to admit that his opinion as an authority must necessarily be of greater value than any we can offer in reply. But its weight is chiefly the outcome of his experience, and in so far as we can approach him in this we find that this same authority is only a more enlightened intelligence and understanding than our own.

Great critical powers are of course far more than mere study and experience. The true critic, we have seen, has a genius or instinct for what is permanently beautiful in art which years of patient labour will not bring. Taste has been admirably defined as Intuition plus Experience. Intuition, unfortunately, comes not by observation. Experience, in the fullest sense of the word, is but slowly won. But apart from the exhaustive study of art, which forms the life's work of the professional art-critic, there is a kind of novitiate in the rudiments of art-teaching which robs authority of some of its terrors, and gives courage and confidence to the student. The trained eye, so essential to the critic, is largely a matter of experience. It must not be thought that too much stress is being laid upon study in discussing the criticism of art. A picture is far more than an exercise for the mind, a book written on a single page, the coloured map of a moment, a lesson on canvas. A great gallery is no mere dictionary of art, useful for reference and study. If this point of view is emphasised here, it is because without it the fuller understanding and pure enjoyment of a picture is wellnigh impossible. And herein the personal point of view has its fullest scope. To arouse the powers of enjoyment, of abandonment to beauty as an end in itself, is the legitimate aim of art. If we look at pictures to understand, it is that thus we may come to enjoy them. It has been said that there has come upon art something of excessive earnestness and effort, out of harmony with its spirit. Pater, one of the most naturally gifted and subtle of modern critics, to whom the love of art was an instinct, a passion, merely emphasised this view when he fancifully but bitterly complained of "people who would never really have been made glad by any Venus fresh risen from the sea, and who praise the Venus of old Greece or Rome only because they fancy her grown now into something staid and tame." Herein at least the individual is unfettered, free to enjoy the fulness of beauty wherever he can find it. He may find it, like Flaubert, in the great masters of the past. "All I ask," he wrote, "is to retain the power of admiring the great masters with that enchanting intimacy for which I would willingly sacrifice all else." Or he may seek it in the masterpieces of his own age, daring to direct an enlightened and whole-hearted enthusiasm upon the best he can discover, even though he may never hope to hear his judgment finally confirmed.

CHAPTER II

CONSIDERATIONS OF DATE

GREAT art, it has been said, is for all time, and is therefore independent of time. It is of all ages, of every land. And if by this we merely mean that the creative spirit in man which produces a picture or a statue is common to the whole civilised world, independently of age, race and nationality, the statement may stand unchallenged.

Looking more closely at the forms under which this spirit manifests itself, there is indeed no end to their variety, and yet each bears a very remarkable family likeness to others produced in the same period and environment. The fact may be verified by visiting any gallery where pictures of many different centuries and schools hang together. There are, indeed, pictures by old masters which strike us by their singularly modern appearance ; but this merely emphasises the truth of the statement. Even the comparatively unpractised eye can generally get within a hundred years of the age of a picture, the acute critic within a decade, and perhaps one of the first questions that suggests itself in looking at a picture is this of the age in which it was painted. There are probably more disappointments in the presence of great and famous works of art through omitting to bear in mind this obvious point of view than from any other cause. All great art is, to a considerable extent, the outcome of its own age, and the circumstances under which it was produced.   It is through forgetting this that we too often expect mature art of a period of tentative endeavour, that we blame Memlinc for lacking the vigour and freedom of Rubens, or Crivelli for the absence of that breadth which characterised Tintoretto and Veronese.   Our standard must vary immediately, and almost unconsciously, according as we are judging of a Primitive of the fourteenth century, of a ripe work of the high Renaissance, or of a painting by one of our own contemporaries.   Every age has its own artistic methods and ideals, to which its painters give expression.   The painters of one age are interested in problems which are neglected by another.

It is obvious that in art there is no law of continuous progress and achievement.   A period of development and florescence is succeeded by one of decline.   A generation of giants gives place to a race of pigmies.   The course of art is rather that of a succession of cycles, in which decay succeeds activity at more or less regular intervals.   A modern French critic has diagnosed the rise of these movements in the art of painting as the result of a number of artists being struck by the same set of ideas.   These men, finding that their thoughts and impressions are shared by them in common with the society in which they live, are encouraged thereby to the greatest activity.   After a time, however, art ceases to be sincere and spontaneous, as the new inspiring ideas which animated them and made the period great lose their freshness and no longer express the general sentiment.   A period of imitation and repetition sets in, and it is this that we call Decadence.   Again, in course of time, men grow weary of imitation.   They launch out once more in other directions, and a new movement begins.

But the new age does not necessarily work on the traditions of the old, nor begin where the other left off. It does not at the outset consciously gather up the threads of all that has gone before. The difficulty experienced by many minds in realising this fact is nowhere better illustrated than in the story of the young artist who, being asked whether he could surpass Fra Angelico, replied that, considering all the progress which had been made since then, the laws of perspective and the mysteries of light and shade which had been mastered, and all the work of subsequent generations, it would be no credit to him if he could not aspire to paint better. " Reasonable, but wrong," was the reply to this argument ; reasonable because were painting a matter of rules and formulae, developing on a line of continuous and unbroken progress, the deduction had been a fair one ; wrong because the whole history of art bears witness to its falseness.

This is not the place to discuss the vexed question whether or no these successive cycles, these periods of alternate rise and decline in the art of painting, when viewed as a whole and from a distance, do or do not make for continuity, for ultimate progress in the art. Is a wider range of activity an advance on one which was narrower, but in its technical qualities more uniformly perfect ? Does modern painting sum up all that has gone before in the manner of a composite photograph and add something of its own, or has it, in spite of its broader vision, neglected and forgotten some of the fundamental principles of pictorial art ? Were the old masters, with their obvious limitations both of matter and manner, consciously rejecting what they conceived to be beyond the reach of painting, or had they merely failed to realise then the full scope and possibilities of the painter's craft ? Has everything possible in painting been attempted or achieved, or are there still new worlds to conquer? Such are some of the questions that naturally arise, questions to which almost every critic will give a different answer. The periods of rise and fall are by no means regular. The upward movement may, as in the case of the Renaissance, take more than two centuries to reach its culminating point. The period of decline, in its turn, may be shorter or longer. In Italy there has been no great art movement since the decadence of the seventeenth century. German art lay fallow for centuries after the decline of the school founded by Dürer and Holbein. A whole wilderness of barren years separates the great Dutch masters of to-day from their ancestors of the seventeenth century. And this state of things is due to the many disturbing elements—political, social and religious—that come in from outside and prevent the regular operation of the principles of action and re-action in art ideas. It seems impossible to maintain that the crest of each wave is higher than that of its prede-cessor, though the advance of civilisation may perhaps tend to shorten the periods of decline.

For most of us the history of painting begins with those crude gaunt altar-pieces bearing the superscription "Early Italian School," and ends with the current year's exhibitions at Burlington House and the Salons. If ex-tremes meet, as it is said, it is surely not here. And when the painting of all the intervening centuries is con-sidered, the necessity of judging of each in the light of its characteristic excellences and defects becomes the more apparent.

With the thirteenth century, and the rise of Giotto and his followers in Italy, a wonderful awakening took place in the world of art. A new tradition in painting was formulated. A reaction set in against the dead and dying

superstitions of the past, and the revived activity in life
and thought created a new spirit in art, full of energy
and vitality, looking to the present rather than the past
for its inspiration.   By the time the fourteenth century
was growing old, the movement had spread widely
throughout Italy.   In drawing, perspective, composition,
colouring and chiaroscuro, the painters of this period
indeed had still almost everything to learn.   The Madonnas and Saints of the early Florentine and Sienese
artists are often almost pathetic in their want of anatomy.
There is little or no modelling, and a total absence of
light and shade; the flesh colours are purely conventional,
the draperies arbitrary.   The scope of painting was
strictly limited.   It was still wholly occupied with depicting the pains and penalties of ecclesiastical heterodoxy,
the dogmas of the Church, and the lives and adventures
of its Saints and heroes.   It was still purely Christian,
and for the most part monkish.   Moreover, it was still
subservient to the requirements of architecture.

In the fifteenth century, however, painting made the
most extraordinary advance.   Not only in Florence and
Siena, but now in Umbria, Lombardy and Venice artists
were springing up with all the vitality and vigour of their
predecessors united to greatly increased technical knowledge.   Learning from successive failures, and striking
out in different directions, with fresh sources of inspiration, new materials and greater freedom of choice, they
pushed steadily on.   The laws of perspective, unknown
to the fourteenth century, were gradually evolved and
applied.   What Giotto had not even dared to attempt
in this direction, Uccello tried and Mantegna achieved.
The study of the nude, inspired by the sister art of
sculpture and the discovery of antique models, was pursued by such ardent students as Pollaiuolo and Signorelli.

Pagan ideals and modes of thought came to rival and, in some cases, temporarily displace those of Christianity.

In the fourteenth and fifteenth centuries too, contemporaneously with this great advance in Italy, the art of painting took root in Germany among the masters of Cologne, and at the same time blossomed forth in unexpected vigour and beauty in the Netherlands. Flemish art, under the brothers Van Eyck, Roger van der Weyden and Memlinc, seemed to need no years of infancy. From what has come down to us we gather that its earliest efforts were bold and confident, its methods elaborate and accomplished. It led the way in portraiture and landscape, leaving Italy for the moment far behind in these directions.

In the sixteenth century the advance was even more rapid and far more general. Italy, which had given birth to the movement, retained her pride of place, and Italian art now reached its fullest maturity. It was a century of marvellous activity and masterly achievement. It might almost seem as though nothing in painting remained to be learned. Never had colour been so boldly and successfully used as by the great Venetian painters Giorgione and Titian, Tintoretto and Veronese. The perfect draughtsmanship of the Florentine masters, Leonardo and Michelangelo, Raphael and Andrea del Sarto, had never before been equalled. In the North Dürer and Holbein inaugurated a Renaissance in Germany at the same time that the great Italian masters beyond the Alps were in their fullest and most splendid activity.

The seventeenth century witnessed a complete change in the distribution of artistic achievement. Italy, the first to rise, was the earliest to decline. She no longer produced, though she still continued to influence. Lightness and grace became triviality and affectation. Strength and grandeur degenerated into heaviness and dullness. Germany too seemed to have outlived her own art. But the Netherlands, with Rubens and Van Dyck, enjoyed a renaissance the more brilliant in that it coincided with the almost total eclipse of Italian art, and Holland gave birth to a school of painters at whose head stand Hals, Rembrandt and Ruysdael. At the same time France, which had hitherto concerned herself more with the patronage of Italian art than with founding a school of her own, gave to the world a style of painting born of classical traditions, initiated by Claude and the Poussins. In this century too Spain, though hitherto almost unknown in the world of painting, brought forth two artists of widely different genius in Velasquez and Murillo; Velasquez, the father of modern painting, Murillo, distinguished by far less originality but possessed of no little charm.

With the advent of the eighteenth century Italian painting, with the exception of such painters of the second rank as Tiepolo and Canaletto, Guardi and Longhi, had almost ceased to be. Spain has but Goya's name on her roll of fame; Germany, Flanders, Holland not one painter of first-rate importance. France, with Watteau and Fragonard, elaborated the art of cultured artificiality on its most charming side, while Chardin sought his inspiration in homely effects of domesticity and still life. And now, when painting elsewhere seemed to have exhausted its resources and lost all spontaneity, England for the first time advanced into the arena, and under Hogarth, Reynolds and Gainsborough enjoyed a late renaissance of her own.

Lastly, in the nineteenth century, the age of industry and commercial activity, we find a general revival of the art of painting throughout Europe. The tendency of nineteenth-century art has been to assert its independence of the centuries that preceded it, to rely no longer on a tradition with which the times were out of touch, to look forward rather than back, to learn from nature rather than from the old masters. Hence its chief characteristic is its endless diversity, its almost unlimited scope, the fearlessness with which it attacks problems unassailed by the painters of any other age. Hence, too, the difficulty of formulating its tendencies, a difficulty enhanced by the close proximity to our own contemporaries which forbids our seeing them in true perspective.

With such fluctuations from century to century it is clear that our standard must vary proportionately. It is not that we can feel equally in sympathy with the products of every age. Our individuality is too strong. Moreover, each age has its peculiar manner, its own triumphs and failures, its characteristic excellences and defects. You do not ask perfection of draughtsmanship or modelling of the fourteenth century, mature landscape art of the fifteenth, advanced realism in style or subject of the sixteenth. You do not go to the seventeenth century for deep religious feeling, or to the eighteenth for *naïveté* and natural charm. But the sense of disappointment and flagging interest that is so often experienced in looking at pictures does not arise from our consciously demanding certain qualities and characteristics of any given century and resenting their absence, but rather in our not knowing what each century has to offer, and therefore failing to recognise whatever special excellence it may possess. It is true in the presence of a great picture we often feel its beauty, its power over us, without a thought of when, where or by whom it was

C

painted. We do not even ask these questions, and certainly we neither know nor care to learn their answers. The function of painting is not to exercise the intellect, but to please the eye. This is true, but it is not the whole truth. There are many pictures which cannot do all this for us, pictures that the eye would pass by but that the mind bids it pause and look again. Moreover, even where we linger most willingly under the sensuous spell of beauty, our knowledge does not freeze or contract our aesthetic appreciation. On the contrary, the student, the connoisseur, is your true enthusiast. He sees farther and tastes longer.

And thus fully to understand a picture we must try to see it with the eyes of the painter's own age, to recognise in his art what were his objects, his ideals, and what the ideals and qualities most revered and prized by his contemporaries. It is when we come to see that every picture should, to some extent at least, be regarded in the light of the time in which it was painted that it becomes clear why the mere imitation of the style of a past age can never produce a great work of art, and the many attempts made of late years, to paint pictures after the manner of Dürer, Holbein, Van Eyck, Filippo Lippi or Gerard Dou are doomed to failure from the outset. The fate of those who thus look back is that of Lot's wife. It is not that the mannerisms and methods of a painter cannot be in part reproduced and even the touch of time rendered again with some exactness, but the life of the picture will be but seeming, the interest forced and false, and the result altogether lacking in all the freshness and spontaneity which form the charm of the old master. Pictures, even by the most gifted modern artists, produced by such a process, are mere phantoms of the Middle Ages. Moreover, these imitators, it has been well pointed out, "have sought to transfer to their pictures not only the beauties but the defects of their great models, forgetting that early masters attract us not on account of their meagre drawing, hard outlines, erroneous perspective and conventional glories, but, on the contrary, in spite of these defects and peculiarities." The truth is that "the most valuable lesson of the past teaches an artist to use the best methods of that past to execute what he wishes to paint, but to wish to paint what he himself sees and feels."

There is one point which cannot be insisted on too strongly in dealing with these questions of chronology in painting. The common tendency to judge of all art, especially of the art of the present, by comparing it with previous art, often results in ignorant and prejudiced antipathy to all innovation or originality. This tendency, however, based on what has been well termed "the traditional spirit of the public," is due not so much to excessive study of the history of the development of art, but to the prevailing idea that between the art of the old masters and that of our own contemporaries there exists a hard and fast line of demarcation ; that the so-called "old masters" are on a different level from the best masters of to-day, belong, indeed, to another category. Nothing is further from the truth. Much of the worship of the old is due to intellectual cowardice begotten of ignorance. The old masters are not always good. The halo with which they are surrounded is often unjustified. Many old pictures dating from the best periods are not to be compared with the productions of modern mediocrity. For in the same way that many of the finest works of the fifteenth and sixteenth centuries have been destroyed by misadventure, so accident has preserved for us others of quite inferior value.   Painting in its broadest aspects preserves from age to age a real continuity.   Styles may alter, but the essentials remain. The painters of to-day will be the old masters of to-morrow.   And so it comes about that there is no phase of modern painting, however startling in its novelty, however audacious and revolutionary in its originality, which cannot be paralleled among the most universally respected of these same "old masters."   Giorgione was in his way as revolutionary as Manet, Rembrandt as Whistler, Hogarth as Madox Brown.   Whenever tradition and only tradition has been the watch word of painting, art has declined, until the inevitable reaction sets in and experiment takes its place.

CHAPTER III

THE INFLUENCE OF RACE AND COUNTRY

ALMOST as important a question as the date of the picture is the nationality of its painter. Whistler indeed has poured scorn upon this idea of nationality, maintaining that art is cosmopolitan. " There is no such thing as English art," he has told us ; "we might as well talk of English mathematics." The paradox is brilliant but the analogy fallacious. The influence of nationality, of physical and political conditions has indeed been somewhat unduly emphasised, especially by the French critic and philosopher, Henri Taine. But it is obvious that the life, character and history of a nation must be to no small degree reflected in its art. Art is inevitably the expression of external conditions, modified though they be by the genius and personality of the artist. The painter's inspiration must ultimately be derived to a large extent from what he sees and hears around him in daily life and from the traditions which he has imbibed from childhood. These he reproduces with more or less of exactness, according to his own temperament and habits. As a rule he takes what is nearest and therefore most familiar. The heavy, phlegmatic type of the native of Holland and the physical features of his country, with its low, level pastures intersected with canals, are faithfully portrayed in Dutch art. So too the sunny skies of Italy, the regular, classical features of her people and the gracious beauties of her landscape are reflected in Italian painting.

But even before we come to the characteristics of nationality, characteristics peculiar to a country or people, there are certain broader distinctions that have had a very real influence on the art of painting, especially during its early history.   Such are the distinctions that at once suggest themselves between the art of Northern and that of Southern Europe.   These are due to causes of infinite variety, differences of race, climate, history and physical features, which cannot fail to influence the art in which they are mirrored.

Roughly speaking, the North of Europe is peopled by a Teutonic, the South by a Latin race.   The reserved, intellectual Teuton differs as much from his vivacious, sensitive Latin cousin as the gray mists and clouds of the North from the brilliant sunshine and clear skies of the South.   The Teutonic nature is reflective rather than imaginative, and less developed upon the sensuous side than the Latin.   This does not imply that it is less absorbed in the problems of art than the other, but only that it approaches them from a different side.   These differences in temperament and character between the Teutons of the North and the Latin-speaking races of Southern Europe are so marked in the literature and manners of each that it would be strange if they were not emphasised in their art.   Nor are they confined to the peoples alone.   They are as pronounced in the climatic and physical conditions under which they live.

In the North the climate is generally cold and damp, the atmosphere hazy.   Long sunless periods accustom the eye to prevailing tones of gray.   Figures are not as it were silhouetted against a background of clear sky, but are seen rather as broad masses of colour and light and shade, losing themselves in a haze of atmosphere. Climate has its effect even upon the medium employed by the artist. Fresco-painting is almost unknown in the North, where the damp atmosphere rapidly destroys all but the most carefully protected pictures. So far from exposing them to the open air, it has even been thought necessary to cover those in our National Gallery with glass, in spite of the grave disadvantages of such a course.

In the South this is in many respects changed. A warmer, sunnier climate and dry atmosphere make fresco suitable even for open courts and cloisters. Many such paintings have retained their original freshness for centuries. Moreover, in the South and especially in Italy the traditions of a classical past, whose remains were scattered over the length and breadth of the country, exercised an influence profound and enduring. The study of the nude was a passion in the country most suited for it by nature. This classicism seems to have affected the painting of the North but little, until in the seventeenth century Italian influence carried it all over Europe. The classical spirit of the South was manifested also in the idealising tendency which characterises Italian art as compared with the greater realism of the North. The principles of selection and generalisation were little understood in Germany and the Netherlands, where a tendency to insist upon particular detail rather than general decorative effect characterised painting throughout the earlier period of its history.

But even within these broader and more general aspects of the art of North and South there are essentially national characteristics distinguishing the art of one country from that of another. These again apply especially, though not entirely, to the art of past generations, and are more clearly to be traced the further we go back in the history of painting. They depend upon the social, political and religious characteristics of the country, upon its types, customs and dress, its physical features, landscape and architecture. The traveller passing from one country into another, even from one province into another, is struck by the marked differences of type that meet him as he crosses the frontier. In the past these physical differences were accentuated by far greater diversity of dress and mode of life than in these days of levelling civilisation. Yet even to-day we can easily distinguish English from German, in spite of their common Teutonic origin, or French from Italian, though both be of Latin race. Although the painter may modify the types among which he lives, he seldom escapes entirely from them. They are as enduring as language itself. We may detect them in any gallery where pictures of different nationalities are hung. Without guide or catalogue it is often easy simply from the types portrayed to decide whether a picture be Italian, Flemish, Spanish or English. No one could mistake one of Jan van Eyck's plain-faced, high-browed Madonnas for any but a Flemish burgher's wife, a class to this day singularly devoid of grace or beauty. Again, how essentially Spanish are Murillo's dark-skinned, black-eyed beggar boys ; and who could mistake the graceful and elegant types of Reynolds, Gainsborough and Romney, for any but well-born English men and women? In Italy, indeed, compounded as she was of many units, the distinction is carried even further. The Florentine differed from the Venetian as though the two cities had varied, not only in forms of government and history, but even in nationality itself. We have but to compare the blonde, massive types of Titian or Palma's models with the slender forms and more intellectual features portrayed by Botticelli, Ghirlandaio or Leonardo. Every country has its own ideal or type of beauty, which its artists help to define. Even in their religious pictures the Italian and Flemish masters chose their models from the men and women among whom they lived. In Filippo Lippi's *Annunciation* in the National Gallery the Virgin and the Angel Gabriel are simply a Florentine youth and maiden of his day, perhaps somewhat idealised. Indeed, Filippo's Madonna is often merely the portrait of his own wife, and Ghirlandaio's frescoes teem with portraits of distinguished contemporaries.

Equally distinctive of each country are the physical features of its landscape and the prevailing style of architecture. The hedge-rows, orchards and green pastures, the thatched cottage and Gothic church, the rolling clouds and fitful gleams of sunshine are as characteristic of England as are the cypress and olive, the vineyards, the tall slender campanile, the blue skies and clear horizons of Italy. Perugino's landscape backgrounds with their steep blue slopes and winding valleys are as truly representative of the hill country about Perugia as are Constable's leafy lanes and homesteads of his beloved Eastern counties. Equally typical are the bare rocks and snowy peaks of the grim Spanish Sierras introduced into the backgrounds of Velasquez and Goya, while Masaccio and Memlinc have perpetuated the tall, steep houses and high gables of their native Florence and Bruges. But nowhere perhaps more than in Dutch art do we feel how great a part the physical features of the country have played. The Dutch masters of the seventeenth century, Van Goyen, De Koninck, Hobbema, Van der Heyden, set themselves with characteristic directness to reproduce every aspect of their low-lying, level pasture lands, intersected by silvery waterways and studded with windmills, their prim red-brick houses and vast whitewashed churches. And it was but natural that this nation, once mistress of the high seas, should have produced also a great school of marine painters.

Equally important in its influence on art was the religion of the country. Modern painting is indeed but little affected by this consideration. Never has art been more independent of religion than at the present day. But its early history proves how profoundly painting was affected not only by the tenets, but also by the forms and ceremonies of the prevailing creed. Herein again some of the broader distinctions between North and South may be traced. The religion of Northern Europe is for the most part, though with some notable exceptions, Protestant ; that of the South, Roman Catholic. In exclusively Catholic countries like Italy and Spain, it is natural that the views of that Church should prevail in their art. The Church deeply colours the life of the people. Its teaching has always made a deliberate and powerful appeal to the senses and emotions. Painting first arose as the handmaid of a Church which preached and taught by its pictures. The Southern mind was stored to the full with legends of the innumerable saints of the Roman Calendar. Even when their virtues and saving powers were no longer respected, their stories and attributes remained familiar. Every church contained numerous altars, above each of which it was the desire and pride of the pious to raise a masterpiece. Thus Church pictures were everywhere in demand, and some of the finest altar-pieces of the Italian Renaissance were executed to the order of wealthy prelates or ecclesiastical bodies, or at the command of one of the great noble families for the adornment of private chapel or public hall. In the same manner, too, the walls of chapel or cloister were covered with frescoes, which should serve the double purpose of instruction and decoration. For the architectural arrangement of the churches of the South, with their endless series of chapels, small windows and abundant unbroken wall-space, gave opportunities to painting unparalleled in the Gothic architecture of the North, with its mullioned windows filled with stained glass and its altarless aisles. In the same way the pageants organised by the ecclesiastical and civic authorities to celebrate the great religious festivals not only accustomed the eye to appreciate the spectacular effect of masses of vivid colour, but when reproduced on wall or canvas still further tended to identify Latin Christianity with the art of painting.

By the time Holland and England had begun to develop their national schools of painting, the Reformation had swept over Europe, cleaving its religious life into two distinct divisions. The Reformed Church had little sympathy with the art of painting, was indeed more than half suspicious of it as an ally of the Roman faith. The ascetic creed of Calvin forbade any appeal to the senses through the medium of music or painting. As a natural result of this feeling, scarcely a suggestion of religious inspiration exists either in English or Dutch art. In both countries painting developed independently of the Church, without its encouragement, but free from its restricting influence. Art patronage in these countries was secular, not ecclesiastical. Their peoples affected no interest in the old monkish tales of the Saints or the legends of the Madonna. It is no wonder then that art was directed into other channels and took other forms, and that portraiture, landscape and genre became the most characteristic and therefore the most favoured. Instead of altar-pieces, we find huge life-size portrait-groups of the Dutch Guilds and Corporations, Regent pictures, as they are called. The finest series, that from the hand of Frans Hals, now adorning the long Municipal Gallery at Haarlem, represents the officers of the guilds of Arquebusiers grouped round their banqueting tables in all the bravery of gala uniform and ceremonial. These are as peculiarly Dutch as the *Fêtes galantes* of Watteau and Lancret, in which elegantly dressed noblemen and ladies dance minuets on the green turf or foregather about a marble fountain, are characteristically French.

Thus, in choice of subject, in methods of treatment, even in such matters as the size of pictures, differences of nationality have been clearly marked, and as each has been the outcome of the special genius and requirements of the nation that produced it, success has never attended the deliberate adoption of the characteristics of one country by the artists of another. The Italian masters and their successors, the Flemish painters of the seventeenth century, were chiefly employed in covering huge wall-spaces or canvases with scriptural, allegorical or mythological subjects. It was only towards the sixteenth century that easel pictures for private houses came into favour in Italy. The Dutch masters used the smallest possible panel or canvas on which to depict the portraits, the landscapes and genre scenes, for which a great demand had arisen.

Vain attempts have been made from time to time to counteract these national and climatic influences. Many of the Flemish artists of the sixteenth century, Mabuse, Bernard van Orley and a host of others, abandoned their native art and flocked to Italy to study that of Rome.

FRANS HALS

OFFICERS OF THE GUILD OF ARQUEBUSIERS

[Haarlem

The results were deplorable from the first. They lost the habits of careful drawing and observation of their predecessors, and gained only in their place an exaggerated melodramatic style that may be recognised at once as the result of an alien influence ill-assimilated. In the same way the huge allegorical and classical pictures of our English academic painters, Haydon, Barry and Fuseli, obviously modelled on Correggio, Raphael, Michelangelo and the great Venetians, are far more ridiculous than sublime. It is as though the artists were attempting to converse in a language wholly foreign to them.

To-day differences of nationality have almost ceased to influence art. Facilities of travel have practically annihilated them. An English artist may find his teacher in Paris and his model in Venice. Two centuries ago, if a painter travelled, it was to Rome, as to the one artistic Mecca. Now he goes everywhere, to Paris, Munich, the East, to study, copy and assimilate whatever influences cross his path. Photography and modern processes of reproduction have increased this denationalising tendency. The change was strikingly illustrated at the Paris Exhibition of 1900. In the Louvre, grouped according to their respective countries, the Italian, Flemish, Dutch, German, French and English pictures need no description to identify their nationality. In the Grand Palais of the Exhibition the names of the same nations appeared over the doors of their respective rooms, but in many cases the most acute critic would have been unable to restore a wandering canvas to its own country. Art from this point of view has indeed become cosmopolitan.

One other consideration, inseparably associated with the idea of locality, has more influence upon our estimate of pictures than is generally understood, the *milieu* in which they are seen. The growth of great representative collections, embracing the works of every country, every school, tends to dull our appreciation of this fact. A picture is happiest in the country in which it was painted. An Italian picture is always something of a foreigner in England or Germany. In Florence it is difficult to tune one's mind to enjoy the fine Dutch and Flemish pictures in its galleries. Indeed only when we have seen the pictures that still remain in their own country can we fully appreciate those in exile.

CHAPTER IV

SCHOOLS OF PAINTING

PICTURES are commonly classified according to Schools. We speak of the Schools of Italy and Spain, of the French and Dutch Schools of painting, including in these general terms a great variety of achievement. The word " School " as applied to painting is, however, used in many other senses, sometimes illogical and always confusing unless the precise meaning attached to each is kept in view. We talk of the English School, the Florentine School, the School of Rubens, the Pre-Raphaelite School, the Impressionist School, the Barbizon School, and finally of a " School-picture." It is obvious that here this same hard-worked term is applied in at least three different senses. School may imply either a geographical division, a personal influence direct or indirect, or a group of artists who have adopted certain definite aims or characteristics.

In its first and most familiar sense, then, the word School implies a geographical limit, usually though not exclusively coextensive with national divisions, and independent of considerations of time. It is as natural to speak of the French School or the English School of painting as of French or English literature. Nationality, as we have seen, plays as important a part in art as in all other departments of life. This is the broadest use of the term School in its geographical sense. For within

the general limits of nationality, there are many minor
divisions based on locality, especially in countries where,
as in Italy and Germany, a number of distinct political
units existed side by side.   In the Middle Ages, the
great period of her artistic energy, the term Italy was
merely a geographical expression, and the label " Italian
School " may be attached to many pictures which, though
they bear a certain family likeness, have little in common.
Thus, when we come to differentiate between the School
of Tuscany and that of Umbria, or between the Sienese
and the Venetian Schools, we are using our geographical
distinction in a narrower sense to imply a district or
town.   Local as well as national characteristics, as we
have seen, are most strongly marked in Italian art.   Only
a few miles separate Florence and Siena, both in the
province of Tuscany.   Yet Florence betrays in her art
that eager spirit of scientific inquiry which ever possessed
her, while the art of Siena, devoid of science, was full of
passionate religious fervour and flowing grace.   Still
more pronounced is the difference between Florentine
and Venetian art.   Even in Dutch art the painters group
themselves into schools according to the cities in which
they worked.   We speak of the Schools of Haarlem,
Leyden, Amsterdam or Utrecht, though these cities are
scarce a Sabbath day's journey apart.   The English, or
more properly speaking the British School, being later
in date, has fewer local subdivisions, though even here
we differentiate between the Schools of Norwich, Newlyn
and Glasgow, each with its distinct characteristics.   In
this case, however, the distinction is perhaps rather that
of chosen aim than of unconsciously expressed local
idiosyncrasy.

Another sense in which the word " School " is used is
to express the personal influence of some great artist

upon his pupils and imitators.   The School or Atelier
system has in our day almost disappeared.   True, we
speak of the School of Burne-Jones or Carolus-Duran,
yet meaning something much less definite than when
under the terms School of Giotto or School of Rembrandt
we sweep in a whole host of unknown and nameless
artists, consciously working on given lines.   In the
Middle Ages, when the artist was less an individual than
a member of a guild with its fixed rules to which he was
bound to conform, the painter had but little scope for
originality unless he possessed more than the ordinary
share of talent.   A young painter in the natural course
of events was apprenticed to an artist of standing and
repute, and put to such menial tasks as the grinding of
colours or the preparing of panel or fresco for his master's
use.   In time small unimportant commissions were in-
trusted to him, which he would execute under direction
and supervision, the master himself perhaps adding the
finishing touches.   A strong family likeness must naturally appear in the works of these pupils, painting under
one influence and bound by the traditions of a common
training.   The more gifted and independent would, however, assert their individuality, and in time set up their
own studios and form their own schools.

Thus the atelier of Giovanni Bellini was the great
training-school for Venetian artists of the fifteenth and
early sixteenth centuries.   To his school belonged Titian,
Giorgione, Catena, Basaiti, Bissolo and a host of lesser
luminaries. Of these, Titian and Giorgione, who possessed
genius of the highest order, passed beyond the Bellinesque
traditions and formed new ones of their own.   They may
be said to belong to the School of Bellini only in the
sense that from him they received the elements of their
art.   Indeed it is often suggested that in his turn,

D

Giorgione's poetical spirit was not without its influence on the master himself. But painters like Basaiti, Bissolo and a crowd of others we may strictly include in the School of Bellini. As his assistants, they even signed their works with his name, and this with no fraudulent intent, the signature merely implying that the picture came from the atelier of the *Capo-scuola*. Many a picture displaying distinct Bellinesque characteristics, yet too poor in execution to be assigned to any known pupil, is simply labelled " School of Bellini," and falls into the category of " School-picture," a convenient term to designate a picture suggesting a master's influence but not to be attributed directly to him or to any one of his known pupils. Criticism is active in assigning these waifs and strays to some newly discovered painter, of whom often little but the name is known.

Rubens had a large school of pupils and assistants, who took their part in almost every great work that came from his studio. It is only in his very early pictures that we see pure Rubens, unadulterated by assistants' work. His fame once made, commissions poured in, and anyone who has merely strolled through the galleries of the Louvre, Munich, Vienna and Antwerp must realise how impossible it were for all these acres of canvas to be the work of one pair of hands. We can only wonder at the brain that could produce so rapidly and the powerful personality that so impressed itself upon others and made them work for him. The system was so openly acknowledged that a sliding scale of payment came into use, so much for a picture or portrait entirely by the artist himself, less where he had painted only the head, and still less where he had merely furnished the sketch and added some finishing touches.

The influence of his master may generally be traced

in an artist's work. It never passes wholly out of his style, though often left far behind as the pupil realises his own powers. Many points which puzzle us in looking at a great painter's work can be traced to some mannerism or habit adopted from his master in the impressionable years of youth. The pupil may surpass his master, as Leonardo surpassed Verrocchio, and Reynolds the prosaic Hudson ; or the teacher may always remain as far above the pupil as Raphael towered over Giulio Romano, or Rembrandt over Bol, Eckhout and Gerard Dou. But the long chain of master and pupil can often be traced for many generations, and the pedigree of such a School as that of Florence drawn with considerable accuracy from Giotto through Masaccio and Ghirlandaio to Michelangelo. But artistic pedigrees are seldom so simple or pure. Cross-currents indeed often disturb the flow of influence. They may come in from altogether foreign sources, as when some pupil, leaving his native city, establishes himself in a new country or city under alien influences, whereby his pupils in their turn will display a double origin. So English painting was influenced by the German Holbein, the Flemish Van Dyck and his successors Lely and Kneller, who preceded the more purely English School of the eighteenth century.

The third sense in which the term School is used is to imply some common characteristic or definitely chosen aim uniting a group of painters, often of different nationalities. In this sense we speak of the Eclectic, the Romantic, the Pre-Raphaelite Schools. The Eclectic School arose in Rome and Bologna in the seventeenth century with the decline of Italian art. All spontaneity in painting had spent itself. Painters now set themselves to imitate the works of the great masters, Raphael, Michelangelo and Correggio. Accepting their names as embodying the noblest achievement in painting, these Eclectics set themselves to select such characteristics from each great master as seemed most worthily to represent him, and by combining these to produce a whole which should be at least as worthy as the sum of the component parts. From Raphael they selected perfection of drawing, from Michelangelo grandeur of conception and mastery of anatomy, from Correggio striking effects of light and shade. It was indeed the apotheosis of conventionality. The only result, it has been said, of this desire to resuscitate the dead was to kill the living.

In this sense also we speak of the Romantic School which arose in France in the nineteenth century in reaction against the prevailing severe, classical style, and the Pre-Raphaelite School in England, which also threw down the glove to the Academy and dared to defy the accepted traditions of generations.

CHAPTER V

THE ARTIST

AS we have seen, the painter may be regarded as one of the units forming a nation at a particular period in its history, and also as a member of a school of artists. But ultimately it will be his own individuality, his personal genius that more than any of these will determine the place he is to hold in the world of art.

To ascertain wherein lies the special individuality of a painter is almost as difficult a problem as to analyse his peculiar charm. We may find a clue to it, however, by comparing the work of some artist with that of his contemporaries, more particularly those of his own school. Certain characteristics will be found in all, some of which may perhaps be traced to a common master. These being deducted, so to speak, from the work of the individual, what remains will represent his own personal style, or to use a current expression, his subjectivity. This fact is summed up in the well-known saying of Buffon, which applies to art as well as to literature : " Le style, c'est l'homme."

The new scientific criticism associated with the name of Morelli is based on these principles, and has been applied with great minuteness to the study of early Italian painting. Just as every individual has his own distinctive handwriting, every author his favourite words and expressions, so every painter has his own characteristic manner of rendering form, by which his works may be distinguished from others of the same school.   Certain forms of hand and ear, of drapery and landscape background are peculiar to each early artist, who on the other hand, in his types and general conception, differs but little from his master and fellow-pupils.   Thus Filippo Lippi's broad type of hand and ear, Paris Bordone's peculiar crumpled folds of drapery, Giulio Romano's full, fleshy upper lip are a kind of stamp, differentiating them from artists whom in other respects they closely resemble. In modern painting of course, with its greater realism, this test would not apply at all.   It is only by a process of comparison and elimination that we can estimate the individual contribution of a painter to the art of his day. However closely he may follow in the footsteps of some older painter or even of a contemporary, if he be worthy the name of artist, his personality cannot fail to impress itself on his art.

A striking example of a painter standing out above his contemporaries, and advancing almost at a bound so far beyond them as to leave them out of sight, is that of Velasquez.   His predecessors and contemporaries were men of little note.   Herrera and Pacheco but for their good fortune in having been his early masters would scarcely claim recognition.   Beyond the fact that Velasquez enjoyed the patronage of a rich and powerful Court and the personal friendship of its sovereign, neither his circumstances nor surroundings seemed to promise greatness, and this makes his achievements the more remarkable.

It is in connection with this question of individuality in art that the problem of personal influence inevitably arises.   The influence of some painters over their contemporaries and successors has been overpoweringly great either for good or evil as the case may be.   It is true that some of the greatest artists, Michelangelo for instance, have had few if any direct pupils associated with them, yet their influence has been none the less profound.   On the other hand the influence of such great masters as Raphael, Titian, Rembrandt and Rubens, each of whom stood at the head of a large school, can scarcely be exaggerated. Of all these, Raphael's perhaps has been the most far-reaching, though not entirely for good.   Of an intensely assimilative nature, he seized and perfected all the best qualities of those with whom he came in contact, yet without sacrificing his own individuality.   It is this perfection of style united to the marvellous fertility of his invention, which makes up his power and charm. While he lived to supply the ideas, his pupils seem to have caught something of his spirit.   When he was dead, there being no possibility of improving upon the technical perfection of his art, and his creative power being no longer available, his followers fell into empty imitation. The name of Raphael has always been one to conjure with, but the true Raphael has been too often obscured by the so-called Raphaelesque.   And in the same way the followers of Michelangelo, unable to comprehend the true spirit of his genius, sought to surpass him by exaggerating his defects.

The influence of a great artist survives in his works long after he himself is dead. We can trace that of Titian in many of the pictures of Van Dyck, Delacroix and Watts.   Rembrandt's works inspired, besides his immediate followers, Reynolds, Wilkie, Lenbach and Israels.   We can feel the impress of Rubens in Watteau, Hogarth, Bonnington and Stothard.   And in thus consciously assimilating the influence of a great master there is no plagiarism, no petty pilfering, unworthy of an artist.

Some light may be thrown on the artist's work by the consideration of his life and character. It is not that his painting necessarily reflects his life, or that his character is any criterion of his art, in spite of Michelangelo's theory that good Christians always paint good and beautiful figures. There are far too many exceptions to the rule. No one would imagine that such a painter as George Morland, who devoted himself almost exclusively to pictures of peaceful, country existence, farmyard and stable scenes breathing the very spirit of rural domesticity, had spent the greater part of his life in towns, and that even in such atmosphere it had been noted for wildness and excess. And it is almost as great a surprise to find that Turner, one of the greatest landscape-painters the world has ever seen, should have been London-born and bred, and have passed his best years within its dingy confines. Vasari roundly accuses Perugino of irreligion, and yet no painter of any age has succeeded in conveying the spirit of Christianity with greater delicacy of sentiment. Other instances equally striking might be quoted to prove the opposite. When we remember the repulsive faces in Adrian Brouwer's pictures and the frequency with which he represented tavern-brawls we are not surprised to hear that he himself died young in consequence of his excesses. And do not Fra Angelico's visions of heaven testify to a life devoted to its contemplation? It were, however, idle to dogmatise on such a subject, and dangerous to argue from even the most tempting analogies.

But in looking at pictures there is no doubt that questions often suggest themselves bearing upon the life and character, the circumstances and surroundings of the painter. What led him to choose the subject of his picture, to treat it as he has? Was it the spontaneous outcome of his genius, owing nothing to any picture before it, like Rembrandt's *Night-Watch* at Amsterdam or Giorgione's *Sleeping Venus* in the Dresden Gallery? Was his motive ambition or rivalry, as when Sebastian del Piombo executed his *Raising of Lazarus* in the National Gallery to surpass the *Transfiguration* upon which Raphael was engaged, or Turner painted with Claude's masterpieces before his mind? Was it to obey the commission of some rich patron, as were Raphael's frescoes in the Vatican, painted for that tyrant of artists, Pope Julius II.? Did he paint as Rembrandt painted towards the end of his life, to keep his creditors at bay and provide for his family, or like Rubens and Reynolds for huge fees that even so could not drive the crowd of fashionable sitters from the door? Did he dash it in red-hot in a fine frenzy of inspiration as Tintoretto or Frans Hals would seem to have worked, or was it as with Leonardo the result of long years of toil, painted touch upon touch, with intervals of irresolution and despair before the end was achieved and the brush laid down? Did the subject of his picture form slowly in the painter's brain, built up piece by piece as the careful studies and drawings of many masters would lead us to suppose, or was it a glimpse of some scene in street or field that painted and framed itself, as it were, in a flash across his mind? Only thus could Whistler and Claude Monet have seized the impressions they delighted to depict.

The subject once selected, the further question arises how far the artist's individuality has made itself felt. All great pictures bear the unmistakable stamp of the personality that created them. It is far more than a mannerism, more even than a strongly pronounced style. The painter may allow much of himself to come into his work or little, and according as he is personal or impersonal we may judge of the man within and behind the artist. Some there are, especially painters of portraits, who so absorb themselves in their sitters that their own identity remains almost hidden. With others it is the reverse. We seem to see the artist as well as the sitter when standing before a portrait by Lotto or Andrea del Sarto, Rembrandt or Van Dyck, Gainsborough or Watts. We need no biography to tell us of the sternness of Michelangelo, of Raphael's blithe serenity, that Hals was a fellow of infinite merriment, Rubens a cavalier, Rembrandt a visionary, Van Dyck a courtier and man of the world, Reynolds a scholar.

How extraordinarily complex are the personalities of some of the greatest masters, how perfectly simple those of others. Michelangelo was architect, sculptor, painter, poet, and supreme in all. Leonardo excelled as painter, sculptor, architect, engineer, chemist and man of letters. Rembrandt is as famous for his etching as for his painting. How simple, on the contrary, and indeed in a sense limited both in style and character, are such early artists as Lorenzo di Credi or Carpaccio, and later the Dutch genre-painters Jan Steen and van Ostade, Metzu and Dou, who were content to paint again and again the same subject in the same surroundings with but slight variation of incident or detail.

No one can fail to have observed, both among painters of the present as of the past, how closely the pictures by each master resemble one another ; how the artist, as it were, forms a peculiar style of his own which shows itself in every work no matter what its subject may be. In this he is following out his own individual way of emphasising a truth or presenting a new point of view. Giorgione's romantic treatment, Rembrandt's mysteries of light and shadow, Gainsborough's feathery touch, Corot's low-toned harmonies, Burne-Jones's ascetic types characterise their work, so that when walking through a gallery we can often recognise by whom each picture has been painted. At the same time due appreciation of this personality in style should discourage the peculiarly unhappy practice of contrasting the excellences of one painter with the faults of another, a comparison which is only unjust to both artists.

Some few painters there are whose fame is greatly enhanced by their great rarity and the little we know of them. The fact that but one or two works from his hand are known to exist will often give an artist a prominence he scarcely deserves. Modern research is continually bringing to light some obscure and forgotten painter in whom our interest is as much antiquarian as artistic.

Another point of view in connection with the artist and his picture is that of the period in his career at which he painted it. Was it a work of his youth, produced before his style was fully formed, or was it born later of a ripe experience? The artistic life of every painter divides itself into periods according to the important events and influences that mould it. We may often recognise them without difficulty in his work. Yet many a master between the outset and the termination of his activity has produced pictures so totally dissimilar, that but for a certain individuality of style it is hard to believe they are from the same hand. The first period is, as a rule, the pupil stage, when the influence of his master is the strongest in his art. The pupil lacks the confidence even if he possesses the power of giving his individuality full scope. The manner and even the mannerisms of his master are ever present to his mind, and reproduce themselves, perhaps unconsciously, in his pictures. With growing experience his own style becomes formed, and after a period of full maturity often shows signs of failing powers and eyesight. There is no better illustration of the gradual growth of the artist's power to its fullest development than in the Municipal Collection at Haarlem, where Hals's seven large portrait-groups hang side by side the whole length of the main gallery. They date from 1616 to 1665, thus covering half a century of the painter's career. Here we may note his style becoming broader and bolder, the colouring at first more daring and then again less pronounced, the posing and arrangement less and less conventional, and the whole treatment freer and more masterful. Rembrandt, whether as painter or etcher, is another striking example of marked and rapid development in style, and it is often difficult to believe that the finished closely-painted pictures of his early years, such as the *Presentation* in the Hague Museum, can be by the same hand that produced the *Bathsheba* in the Louvre, or the broadly conceived and vigorously executed portraits of the *Syndics* in Amsterdam. There are indeed some few remarkable exceptions to the rule that the painter tends to grow broader in style as he advances. The later works of Gerard Dou—his famous *Femme hydropique* in the Louvre and his *Jeune mère* at the Hague, painted towards the close of his life —are perhaps the most highly finished of his pictures.

How closely the periods of development in an artist's career correspond with changes in his surroundings is illustrated in the work of Van Dyck. His first period as pupil and assistant of Rubens at Antwerp shows him strongly under this overpowering influence. His portrait of *Van der Geest* in the National Gallery, painted at this time, used actually to be attributed to Rubens, and has only lately been correctly ascribed to the pupil. His second period opens with his visit to Italy, where he painted that magnificent series of Genoese portraits which betray the influence of Titian, and for some years after his return to Antwerp the spell of Italian colour and distinction possessed him. The last period is that of his sojourn in England as painter to the Merry Monarch and the court of gallant Cavaliers and their fair ladies, where his natural instinct for elegance and refinement found full expression. So far did the gay painter associate himself with the spirit of his adopted land, that his series of English portraits in no wise suggest a foreign origin.

Just as in certain years of his life an artist may produce most of his finest work, so too he will have his most inspired and successful moments. And the obvious fact that his work will vary in quality—good, better and best—has been adduced to prove the fallacy of arguing that a disputed work must not be attributed to a famous artist on the ground that it is not good enough for him. Yet surely the test is as fair as any other; it is a question of degree. Given a great reputation based upon works of undoubted authenticity and splendid merit, it is as reasonable to suppose that the artist would not have been responsible for an absolutely inferior picture though superficially in his manner, as to reject the attribution of a masterpiece to a worthless artist on the ground that he could never have risen to such heights. At the same time even the greatest painters have their comparatively uninspired moments, and to expect nothing but masterpieces from an acknowledged master is to court disappointment.

CHAPTER VI

THE SUBJECT

PICTURES are more often looked at from the point of view of the subject they represent than from any other. It is so frequently the first consideration to enter the mind of the spectator that it is idle to regard it as of little or no consequence. At the same time there can be no doubt that the importance of the subject is often absurdly exaggerated, and it is equally certain that it tends to diminish in proportion as our aesthetic appreciation increases.

In early art the subject was from necessity the first consideration for both painter and public. Painting had other purposes to serve besides the aesthetic. Pictures were painted to preach and teach, to warn and encourage, to tell stories and record events. An altar-piece destined for a particular chapel must depict some scene from the life of the saint to whom the building was dedicated. Frescoes upon the wall of Municipal Palace or Council Chamber would naturally represent some special diplomatic or military triumph of the city, or an allegorical conception of its Government. Later, when easel pictures were designed for the adornment of private houses and painting became so cheap as to be within the reach of even the middle classes, the artist was free to paint whatever he desired, limited only by the size of his panel or canvas and the nature of his medium.

To-day the tendency is rather to undervalue the importance of the subject as such, to insist upon the supreme value of its treatment, and to lay stress upon the fact that any subject, however trivial, ugly, even revolting, may in the artist's hands be transformed into a thing of beauty. Carried to its extreme such appeal to the senses through form and colour alone, without reference to the intellect, would differ but little from that made by a wall-paper or a fine piece of embroidery, both often beautiful in colour and design. But the intellectual or moral interest cannot be wholly lost sight of in a picture, which is not merely an arrangement of lines and colours, beautifully and harmoniously combined, and pleasing the eye by their order and variety. All art is essentially human, and must appeal to what is conveniently if illogically termed the human side of our nature. To do so it must represent a subject of human interest. It is a question of compromise. There is no doubt that an exaggerated importance has often been attached to the mere subject. Even the paradox that to the public a picture is interesting in proportion as it is antipictorial scarcely goes too far.

The first question then to ask ourselves, when looking at a picture, is whether the subject be treated pictorially. Has the artist set himself to paint a picture, and not merely to illustrate a subject by copying a model? Has the subject passed through the fire of his imagination? If it fail under this test it fails in everything essential, a fact which cannot be too strongly insisted upon. A picture is no picture unless it be pictorial. As applied to modern art especially this truism is constantly over-looked by those who begin by criticising pictures and end in buying them. We cannot therefore wonder if even the painter tends to lose sight of this principle or consciously abandons it for a more lucrative and successful practice, for to paint pictorially demands the most intimate knowledge of nature, not to be come by without patient study. Much modern painting fails because it is illustrative and nothing more, because in telling a story it forgets to please the eye, because it appeals to sentiment alone, and has no sensuous or aesthetic charm, no true artistic beauty. There is no need to multiply examples. Each year's Academy is full of such pictures, possessing perhaps some suggestion of pathos, humour or even dramatic intention, but failing in all else.

In painting then, the subject, though of interest and importance, is not the primary consideration. Taking a wide view of painting, the achievements of its greatest periods bear this out. When painting has accomplished most the mere subject has occupied the artist least. In periods of artistic mediocrity it comes again into prominence, as though seeking to make us forgetful of shortcomings in treatment and technique.

What then are these pictorial qualities which a picture must possess? Obviously qualities of line, colour and chiaroscuro, and their ordered and harmonious disposition. Besides these there is the actual manipulation of the colours, what has been called " the interest of pure paint," which appeals so strongly to the modern critic and too little to some modern painters. With these means at his command the painter approaches his subject. His treatment of it will depend on his own temperament and training. How unimportant may be the subject he selects we have already seen. Look at some genre piece of the best Dutch period. It may be

almost devoid of intellectual interest and possess no
moral significance whatever.   The painter was as conscious of the fact as is the spectator of to-day, but he
chose his subject not for its interest or importance, but
because he saw its pictorial possibilities, and seized the
opportunity of depicting some beautiful effect of light,
some harmony of colour, some felicity of composition,
some grace of line.   As such it made a picture for him,
and a picture, an object of pleasure for the eye, it will
always remain, though it be after all but a ragged
beggar or the interior of a tradesman's shop that he
paints for us.   Look at some picture by A. van Ostade
of a village inn, where a group of rough peasant fellows
sit drinking at their ease.   The panel glows with rich
though subdued colouring, the tone is exquisitely quiet
and harmonious, the composition marvellously skilful.
The incident is an everyday one, common enough in
Holland as elsewhere.   Van Ostade did not seek to
attach any sentimental interest to his group, nor to
excite our sympathy for what he at least must have
considered a harmless form of relaxation.   The subject
is his servant.   But something in this commonplace
theme caught his eye, delighted his colour-sense, and in
his hands became a picture.   Contrast with this the
comparatively unpictorial treatment of many English
and German genre pictures, in which it is evident that
the artist's chief aim is to tell a story, and to tell it as
charmingly and sympathetically as he is able.   The
subject is his master.   He conceives it in his mind
and then sets himself to paint a group to illustrate it,
under the mistaken belief that painting is literature
masquerading in disguise.   His picture may have an
intellectual, perhaps a moral interest, but it too often
lacks the sensuous charm which is the essence of pictorial

E

art. In a word it is unpictorial. We feel this strongly when looking at the genre scenes by Collins, Newton and Leslie in the South Kensington Museum; still more in the Museum at Brussels where are exhibited the pictures of that "philanthropic ranter" Antoine Wiertz.

But admitting the subject of a picture to be of comparatively slight importance it is nevertheless often of considerable interest. The choice of subject is very much a matter of the age in which the artist paints. Every age requires a range of subjects peculiar to itself, and within these again the dictates of fashion play a part. Broadly speaking the subjects demanded in the fourteenth century were legends of Saints and Madonna, and scenes from the Old and New Testaments. The next two centuries added to these last allegorical and mythological extravagances, illustrations from the poets and, above all, portraiture; while in the seventeenth, landscape and genre subjects and portraiture took the place of the older religious painting. The eighteenth century was the age of portraiture and historical painting, while the nineteenth, insatiable and all-embracing, appears to have taken the whole world for its province and made all subjects its own. There would seem to be nothing on the face of the earth which the painter has not at some time or another chosen to paint. Every age is represented, every country, every race, every season, every hour of day and night. Hardly a story has been told in prose or verse that has not been retold a hundred times in paint.

But although such wealth of subject is at his disposal, the painter's choice therein is limited by his powers. Turner was right to avoid as far as possible figure painting, in which he was fully aware of his weakness. The

custom of two artists collaborating in the painting of a
single picture arose either from the one painter's conscious
want of ability in some particular direction or from his
recognition of his collaborator's conspicuous pre-eminence
therein.   Collaboration was a recognised practice in the
Netherlands.   Even Ruysdael and Hobbema employed
figure painters to relieve their landscapes.   Rubens col-
laborated with Jan Breughel and Snyders, Cuyp with
Van der Neer, Wynants with Adrian Van der Velde.
Some painters indeed were masters of every kind of
subject.   Rembrandt was one of these giants of a hundred
hands.   Rubens was equally at home with religious
pictures, court scenes, battle-pieces, landscapes, portraits,
classical and allegorical themes.

Yet for all this wealth of material to choose from, artists
have often painted subjects which at first sight might
appear the most unpromising.   But for his strong artistic
instinct and wonderful colour-sense, Rembrandt could
never have made a picture out of so ghastly a subject
as the *Anatomy Lesson* at the Hague, or his *Flayed Ox*,
seen perhaps in some butcher's shop near his home
there.   It is in allusion to Rembrandt that Mr. Colvin
has pointed out the significance of the fact that this
great Dutch master "succeeded in making as wonderful
pictures out of spiritual abjectness and physical gloom
as the Italians out of spiritual exaltation and shadowless
day."

How far all subjects are equally suited to pictorial
treatment is a question too wide to be attempted here.
The tendency of the inferior painter is to attract attention
by the sensational nature of his subject rather than by
the mastery of its treatment.   Indeed, many artists have
sometimes erred by representing scenes either so painful
or so coarse that the taste is offended, however skilful

the rendering and treatment.   The tortures and torments of Saints and Martyrs rendered with faithful realism by the old Flemish painters, and in melodramatic effusiveness by the later Italians, illustrate this, in the same way as the exquisitely painted panels of vulgar scenes by the great Dutchmen Brouwer and Jan Steen.   Indeed, the whole Dutch School is an example of the triumph of pictorial skill over subject.   The types are nearly always ugly, sometimes even grotesquely deformed ; yet the pictures produced are often masterpieces of painting, delighting the eye by their colour and appealing to us by their warm sympathetic treatment of life.

For all the variety of subject at the painter's command, broadly speaking it may be said that all pictures fall into certain well-defined groups, and each of these again into smaller subdivisions.   Charles Lamb has laughingly pointed a warning finger at " that rage for classification by which in matters of Taste at least we are continually perplexing instead of arranging our ideas."   The danger lies rather in arguing by analogy from one class to another than in the classification itself.

The three principal groups under which subjects may be classified are Historical, Landscape and Genre ; while Historical pictures may be again subdivided into strictly Historical, Religious, Mythological and Allegorical, and Portraits.   It is not contended that this division is a strictly scientific one.   Nor will it be found that every picture falls directly and naturally under one of these headings.   On the contrary, pictures will readily suggest themselves that seem to be on the borderland of two or even three groups, but exceptions like these leave the whole principle of classification quite unaffected.

VELASQUEZ

THE SURRENDER OF BREDA

Laurent photo]

[Madrid

CHAPTER VII

HISTORICAL PAINTING

I N Historical painting it is inevitable that the subject represented should play an important part. By its associations, by its appeal to the memory or the emotions it should contribute an element of human interest for which the picture as a work of art is the richer. But even here to illustrate an incident is not the sole object of the historical painter. It is not his aim to focus into a moment of vision the pages of a book of history or biography, as in a kind of artistic shorthand. The painter and the historian have this indeed in common that each presents and perpetuates some great or small event of interest ; but here the likeness ends. The painter has not merely to chronicle facts, but to present them in such pictorial fashion as will appeal to the eye and the imagination.

The first group of Historical subjects will include all pictorial representations of historical scenes and events, past or present. It embraces such pictures as Veronese's *Family of Darius at the feet of Alexander*, *The Surrender of Breda* by Velasquez, Terburg's *Peace of Münster*, Copley's *Death of Chatham*, Makart's *Entry of Charles V. into Antwerp* and the *Diamond Jubilee Procession*. Thus the painter will select a subject from contemporary history, a scene of which he may even have been an eye-witness, or from a past which he must reconstruct for himself from descriptions and his own imagination. Veronese chose the humiliation of the Persian monarch ? less for the interest he felt in its historical significance than for the opportunity it gave him to depict a scene of gorgeous colour and pageantry. It was not the triumph of Greek civilisation over the Barbarian that inspired him, but the vision his imagination conjured up of a royal family in robes of state before a victorious general and his staff. Little did he care for historical accuracy of costume or *mise-en-scène*. The wife and daughters of the Persian king are no Orientals in flowing draperies, but golden-haired Venetian ladies attired in the costume of the sixteenth century, and the setting is an Italian palace. In this Veronese was only following the dictates of his art. Most painting representing past events is full of the frankest anachronism. This is equally striking in the religious painting of the fifteenth and sixteenth centuries. It is quite usual to find saints of every age and country gathered round the Madonna, or assembling at the foot of the Cross ; and the city of Jerusalem or Bethlehem is often represented by the gabled houses and pinnacled walls and towers of the painter's own town.

Historical painting may thus be so only in name, or in ' the sense that it records the life, architecture and costume of the painter's own country and period rather than of the one he is ostensibly portraying. For a painter is not an antiquarian. We value historical accuracy less than more purely artistic qualities. At the same time modern painters like Leighton and Alma Tadema have combined antiquarian research and fastidious accuracy of detail with artistic presentment. In the eighteenth century the old anachronisms were inverted. The prevailing taste was entirely classical. Painters in quest of the Grand Style insisted that the figures of contemporary statesmen or warriors should be clad in Greek or Roman costume. In the battle-pieces of Gérard and Girodet the soldiers of the Napoleonic Empire are represented as Roman warriors armed with spear and shield instead of musket and pistol, and posed in heroic attitudes, suggestive rather of statuary than of the modern battlefield. It was West who, in his *Death of General Wolfe*, painted in 1768, first dared in defiance of the prevailing artistic canons to dress his heroes in modern regulation uniform. This innovation created not only a scandal but an artistic revolution. It was indeed significant of the new era of naturalism which succeeded to the pseudo-classical *régime*.

Historical painting includes, besides strictly historical scenes, all religious, mythological and allegorical subjects. It is difficult to estimate how much of its inspiration painting owes directly to the Bible. There is scarcely an incident either in Old or New Testament or in the Apocrypha lending itself to pictorial treatment, which has not been rendered again and again by successive artists with infinite variety. Until our own time almost every such scene had its traditional mode of representation, generally more or less faithfully followed.

Religious subjects were, for the most part, produced before the seventeenth century, at a time when painting was still closely allied to the Church. Mediaeval painters received most of their commissions from churches and monasteries, where sacred subjects alone were permissible. Consequently every collection of their pictures is full of renderings of the Madonna and Child, legends of Saints and of the Monastic Orders, scenes from the Passion, visions of Heaven and Hell. Archangels and Apostles, Saints and Martyrs, whose uniform sanctity of expression might have caused serious embarrassment to the faithful, were distinguished by their historical or legendary attributes. The four Evangelists may be recognized by their emblems—the angel, the lion, the bull and the eagle. St. Catherine of Alexandria stands beside her broken wheel, St. Laurence carries his gridiron, St. Nicholas of Bari his golden balls, St. Francis is known by his brown habit and the stigmata, St. Dominic by the black and white dress of his Order and the lily he often holds, while the central figure is generally the Madonna enthroned with the Christ-child. The whole Christian Hagiology passes before us in robes of state. The types may vary endlessly, but the traditional forms and composition are preserved with astonishing pertinacity to the very end of the fifteenth century. The Venetian painters of the Renaissance did indeed evolve a new and less formal setting for the religious picture in the Santa Conversazione. Dispensing with throne and architectural background they paint the Virgin and attendant Saints gathered picnic-wise under pleasant trees in charming landscapes. Such pictures, frank representations of Italian life of the day, are sacred only in name.

From the Old Testament those incidents were generally chosen which corresponded with the teaching of the Church, or anticipated that of the Gospels. In the wall-frescoes in the Sistine Chapel the whole scheme is based on the representation of type and anti-type, Pintorrichio's *Circumcision of the Sons of Moses* facing his *Baptism of Christ*, Cosimo Roselli's *Moses receiving the Law on Mount Sinai* over against his *Sermon on the Mount*. A favourite subject was the story of the Creation and Fall of Man, which, like that of St. Sebastian's Martyrdom, gave to early painters the rare opportunity of depicting the nude.

In our own day, indeed, there has been something of a return to favour of this class of religious subject, characterised, however, by the abandonment of traditional forms and *naïve* anachronisms, and aiming rather at literal and historical accuracy of type and setting. Such pictures as those of Tissot are interesting to the antiquarian and Biblical student, but as artistic productions they are of little value. For the most part the kind of artistic temperament which in the fifteenth century would have chosen to depict the Annunciation, Crucifixion or Assumption is now directed towards allegorical or mystical subjects in which the artist seeks to embody in sensuously beautiful form some definitely moral or metaphysical idea.

Subjects taken from Greek and Roman mythology have been appreciated for their pictorial possibilities by imaginative painters of all times and countries. The amours of Jove, the labours of Hercules, the trials of Psyche, have proved a perpetual source of inspiration. The highly cultured Italian of the Renaissance, with his passion for antiquity, delighted to represent the loves and hates, the exploits and escapades of Gods and Goddesses, the adventures of Nymph and Dryad, Centaur and Satyr. This passion has since spread to every land, and still inspires a considerable part of modern art, which, however, instead of searching the classics for fresh incidents, seeks rather to retell the oldest myths in the most modern way.

Allegorical subjects found favour somewhat early in the history of painting, though the difficulty they offered of representing intelligibly a more or less obscure idea confined them to the simplest forms. Ambrogio Lorenzetti's great allegorical frescoes of *Good and Bad Government* in the Town Hall at Siena, with the gigantic figure symbolising the Government of that city, surrounded by female forms personifying Peace, Justice and other virtues, explains its elaborate intention by the aid of lettered scrolls. Giotto's allegories of *Hope* and *Despair*, *Justice* and *Injustice*, *Faith* and *Inconstancy* in the Arena Chapel in Padua are so much simpler and more direct that they do not need their inscriptions to make their meaning clear. The exact interpretation of Botticelli's *Allegory of Spring*, in the Academy at Florence, still baffles the art historian. The allegories of the Venetian painters Veronese and Tintoretto centred for the most part round their native city. Venice is represented everywhere as a beautiful woman in gorgeous robes, attended by symbolic figures of arts and industries, or celebrating diplomatic or military triumphs. Rubens often selected purely allegorical subjects for some of his greatest canvases. His great Marie de Medicis series in the Louvre shows him attempting to combine historical with allegorical treatment. The eighteenth century saw the culmination of this love of allegorical expression. The vast canvases showing the apotheosis of this or that monarch, lifted in pompous ecstasy heavenwards, with virtues supporting the royal person and the Muses singing his praises or chronicling his achievements, have no imaginative beauty to atone for their faults of execution. In modern painting allegory is chiefly used by artists with either spiritual or else merely mystical tendencies. Watts's allegories of *Love and Life*, *Hope*, *Mammon*, *Love steering the Boat of Humanity* are treated with simplicity of design and a fervour of feeling which proclaim the preacher behind the artist.

CHAPTER VIII

THE PORTRAIT

PORTRAITURE, though included under historical painting, is so important and universal as to demand rather fuller consideration. As a distinct branch of painting it is as old as the art itself. From the days of the ancient Egyptians at least we can discern a craving on the part of the individual that his features shall be perpetuated by the skill of the painter no less than by the cunning of the sculptor. This very human instinct it is that accounts for the rise of a class of artists who, like Scott's Dick Tinto, " levy that tax upon the vanity of mankind which they cannot extract from their taste and liberality."

The fine portrait heads discovered in much of their original freshness upon the mummy cases of seventeen centuries ago, of which examples may be seen in the National Gallery, express feelings common to every age, though the power to embody them in paint has often been wanting. When we come to the Middle Ages we find the Italians of the fourteenth century painting types rather than individuals. Every artist for a century after Giotto adhered to a certain facial type. The power of differentiating individuals which is the basis of all portraiture first made its appearance in art in a subordinate form. The painter when representing a group of figures in the background of some religious picture would often introduce his own portrait or that of some distinguished friend or contemporary. To this fact we owe the existence of many of the most precious early portraits, including those of Dante and his friends in the Bargello at Florence attributed to Giotto. This practice became quite usual in the fifteenth century. Benozzo Gozzoli and Botticelli introduced portraits of the chief members of the Medici family into their pictures of the *Adoration of the Magi*, while Ghirlandaio peopled his frescoes with Florentine celebrities and beauties of the day. In one of the frescoes of the *Last Judgment* at Orvieto, Signorelli represented himself and Fra Angelico, who had previously painted in the same chapel, as spectators. In the North too, Hubert van Eyck introduced his own portrait and that of his brother Jan among the Just Judges on the wing of his great Ghent *Adoration*.

Again, it was not unusual for the donor of an altarpiece to commemorate his own piety by stipulating that his portrait, and even those of his wife and family, should be incorporated in the picture which he was offering to appease Holy Church or some exacting patron saint. Familiar instances of these religious pictures with the donor will readily suggest themselves. Perhaps the earliest occurs in the altar-piece painted by Giotto for Cardinal Stephaneschi, now in the Sacristy of St. Peter's. In some instances the donor would appear inconspicuously in a corner of the picture, as in Filippino's *Vision of St. Bernard* in the Badia at Florence; in others he plays an actual part in the scene, as where Memlinc painted Brother John Floreins kneeling before the Child in the *Adoration of the Magi* at Bruges, or Carpaccio represented the Doge Mocenigo in his votive picture in the National Gallery. Sometimes the whole family of

FILIPPINO LIPPI

Alinari photo   (*Badia, Florence*

VISION OF ST. BERNARD

the donor is introduced either in the centre or upon the wings, as in Holbein's *Madonna* of the Burgomaster Meyer at Darmstadt, or in the great triptych of the *Nativity* by Hugo van der Goes, now in the Uffizi. Even Rubens painted on the wings of the altar-piece commissioned by Nicholas Rockox at Antwerp the portraits of the patron and his wife.

The custom of painting the individual for his own sake without other pretext soon found general favour, and some of the earliest mediaeval portraits that have come down to us date from the fifteenth century and are the work of the Italian and Flemish masters, Uccello, Ghirlandaio, Piero della Francesca and Gentile Bellini, and of Jan van Eyck and Memlinc. Many of these early Italian portraits are in profile, clear cut against a dark background, suggesting the influence of the portrait medals of the period. The difficulties of the full or three-quarters face were not attempted until somewhat later, Mantegna's portrait of *Cardinal Scarampi* at Berlin, painted about 1460, being perhaps the earliest. The Flemish portrait heads on the other hand were generally painted either in full or three-quarters face.

The art of portraiture made great advances in the sixteenth century, becoming now free to develop unfettered by exigencies of composition and space. The "New Manner" with its greater breadth and fluency made itself felt. We no longer find the somewhat stiff representation with firm hard outlines and general tightness of execution, but a more natural, lifelike rendering, fuller modelling, greater naturalism of flesh-painting. The spirit of portraiture accorded well with that of the Renaissance, with its insistence upon individuality and craving for fame and immortality. Thus it came about that the introduction of portraits into historical and religious pictures, so common in the fifteenth century, was gradually abandoned by later artists in favour of the independent portrait.   The older practice was not, however, entirely given up.   Titian and Veronese, supreme masters of portraiture, used it also to enhance the interest of their altar-pieces and religious pictures by introducing celebrated contemporaries.   In Titian's *Pilgrims of Emmaus* in the Louvre, Charles V. and Philip II. figure in the parts of Pilgrim and Servitor, and among the guests and musicians in Veronese's *Marriage of Cana* in the same gallery appear Francis I., Mary of England and other notabilities, besides the painter himself with Titian and Bassano.   Even in our own day this practice is not unknown.   Millais echoed the old tradition when he brought portraits of friends and relations, his father, the two Rossettis, F. G. Stephens and others into his *Lorenzo and Isabella* in the Liverpool Gallery.   Besides thus introducing famous personages a painter often took himself or his wife and children as his models.   Filippo Lippi, Andrea del Sarto and Rubens continually painted their wives in the part of Madonna or Saint.   Rembrandt's poverty and waning popularity towards the close of his life obliged him to paint himself and members of his family in lieu of other models.   In the absence of commissions artists can always resort to painting their own portraits, and this perhaps accounts for Rembrandt's numerous versions of his own features.

In painting a portrait there are two considerations, its likeness to the original and its artistic effect.   The first involves the question of Truth, the second that of Beauty, and on his power of combining them depends the painter's success.   It is no little that is demanded of him.   He must be able to make a pleasing picture of the plainest face, and yet the picture must be so close to the original

MRS. SIDDONS AS "THE TRAGIC MUSE"

GAINSBOROUGH

MRS. SIDDONS

that nothing of the sitter's individuality is lost. The question of truth must be tested by independent eyes, for the sitter can never be an adequate judge of his own likeness. But he must do more than faithfully reproduce the colour of hair or eyes, the contours of cheek and chin, the texture of face and hands ; he must be something of a psychologist to read the character, the very soul in the face. He must interpret, not merely copy. And to achieve beauty as well as truth his own genius will come into play, his own individuality will be acting upon that of his original. Thus the personality of painter and of sitter will be in perpetual balance, and on their nice adjustment the quality of the picture will depend. It is just because of this part played by the artist that no two painters ever see or present their model in exactly the same manner, any more than they will describe the same event in the same words. The portrait, therefore, becomes the individual interpretation of a man or woman, not a mere facsimile, such as a photograph can offer.

A good example of this may been seen in the various renderings by some of the greatest artists of the eighteenth century of the famous actress Mrs. Siddons. In Sir Joshua Reynolds's pictures in Grosvenor House and the Dulwich Gallery, she is represented as the Tragic Muse, half woman, half goddess, posed in a magnificent attitude suggestive of Michelangelo. In the National Gallery we have two renderings of her, one by Gainsborough, one by Lawrence, but no two portraits could be more dissimilar in their whole conception and feeling. Gainsborough's *Mrs. Siddons* reflects something of that dignified melancholy which distinguishes all his portraits and is the direct impress of his own temperament. The portrait by Lawrence is conceived in a far less intellectual vein. The flesh-tints are brilliant, and the face has much of that seductive charm which in his hands was apt to degenerate at the cost of character into mere prettiness. Here then we have three portraits of one woman, all of them faithful likenesses yet all different, and this difference is due to the personality of each artist as he interpreted the form he saw before him through the medium of his own imagination.

But while it is true that a portrait reflects something of its painter, the degree in which he will render the individuality of his model varies greatly. Some portrait-painters have been unable to escape from a type of their own and read into every face their preconceived ideal. As a result there is a strong resemblance between all their portraits. Van Dyck gave something of his own natural elegance and distinction to every sitter, to Flemish burgher as to English nobleman. Look only at the hands in his portraits and you will find them always small and delicate with long tapering fingers. It is seldom that he took the trouble to individualise them. They may perhaps give the painter's idea of what hands should be, but they are not those of his sitter. Romney went even further in this almost mechanical repetition. In many of his portraits the lack of individuality is woefully apparent. His women are all sisters, his men cousins at the farthest, the same shaped eyes, the same curling lips do duty in countless faces like so many studio properties. There are always of course certain obvious points of resemblance between portraits of the same period, that depend to a great extent on superficial and accidental likenesses of dress and attitude, the fashion of wearing the hair, or the kind of background chosen. But with many of these highly subjective painters, it is a matter of type rather than of fashion.

In some portraits, on the other hand, it is clear that

VAN DYCK

[St. Petersburg

PHILIP LORD WHARTON

MAN WITH A PINK

the sitter has been viewed impersonally, objectively. The artist has aimed at representing faithfully what he saw before him, though in the actual painting he must always retain his own methods. The earlier portrait-painters as a rule aimed more directly at fidelity to nature than those of a later period. Consider for a moment such a portrait as that of Jan van Eyck's *Man with a Pink* in the Berlin Museum, so wonderfully etched by Gaillard. Every crowsfoot and wrinkle, every crease and furrow left by time or thought is reproduced with almost microscopic accuracy. We see every detail of face and hands as we should see them in the original if we peered closely into them, taking in but a small portion of the surface at a time. The full-length portraits of *Arnolfini and his Wife* in the National Gallery by the same artist illustrate a like relentless fidelity to the original. This plain woman and her gaunt figure of a husband stand there exactly as they stood to be painted. Dürer and Holbein show something of the same fidelity, the same scrupulously fine handling. In Dürer's portrait of *Michael Wolgemut* in the Munich Gallery the unseen window-bars of the room are reflected in the pupils of the eyes, and in that of *Holzschuher* in the Berlin Museum, you can almost count the hairs of the long flowing locks. Among the great portrait-painters, perhaps none has kept the individuality of his sitter more sternly before him than Velasquez. Look only at his *Admiral* in the National Gallery or the *Lady with a Fan* in the Wallace Collection. These searching portraits make their originals realities for us as though we had seen them in the flesh. The portraits of Rembrandt and Hals too are superbly individualised.

It would seem that this fidelity to nature might lead to the neglect of what is, after all, the essential in a por-

F

trait as in every picture, that it please the eye by some quality of beauty. It might be objected that while in portraiture, if anywhere, the subject is of primary importance, if the original be ugly, mean or deformed, the picture can never become a great work of art or satisfy the natural desire for beauty. From this point of view the most that could be expected of such a portrait is that it should be of historical or personal interest as reminiscent of the sitter. If this reasoning were correct, the head of an old man with hideous bulbous nose, surpassing even that of Cyrano, could not fail to repel the eye. Yet this is exactly Ghirlandaio's subject in his wonderful portrait in the Louvre of an *Old Man* looking lovingly down upon his grandson, a portrait which wins and charms by its refinement and sweetness of expression. We cannot help believing it to have been a faithful likeness. We know that it makes a beautiful picture. Velasquez puts the matter beyond all doubt in his portraits of *Philip IV.* and *Innocent X.*, the king's perhaps the coldest and least sympathetic face known to secular history, the Pope's one of the most crafty in the whole line of Pontiffs. Yet there are no finer portraits, no more splendid works of art in the history of painting. Even his Court Dwarfs, thickset, stunted abortions, with heavy animal faces, compel admiration as pictures, as do Rembrandt's old Jewish shop-keepers, suspicious, greedy, mean if the painter has read their character aright, but transformed by the magic of his brush to marvels of art.

We have seen that the Flemish and German portrait-painters of the fifteenth and sixteenth centuries rendered with faithful and minute accuracy the features of those who sat to them, producing portraits of striking realism and characterisation. The great Italian painters of the

PORTRAIT OF HOLZSCHUHER

PORTRAIT OF AN OLD MAN

VELASQUEZ

Laurent photo]   [*Prado, Madrid*

PHILIP IV. ON HORSEBACK

Cinque-Cento carried the art still further. They insisted less on reproducing every line and wrinkle, every hair, with minute exactness, but painting with greater breadth and freedom they combined a masterly rendering of character with a splendour of decorative treatment unknown to the earlier painters. Raphael's *Pope Leo X.*, Titian's *Man with a Glove* in the Louvre, Lotto's soul-searching portraits, Tintoretto's Doges, Veronese's Grandees rank among the masterpieces of the world. They were succeeded by the painters of the North, and in the seventeenth century the greatest names are to be found in the ranks of the Dutch and Flemish masters. Rubens and Van Dyck indeed link themselves with their southern predecessors, combining in their portraits something of the vigorous realism of the North with the freedom and splendour of the great Italians. In Holland there being no demand for religious art painters were free to gratify to the full the desire of the republican burghers to see themselves perpetuated in paint. Particularly in demand were the life-sized portrait-groups, representing the members of guilds or governors of hospitals and almshouses, which are now such a striking feature of Dutch picture-galleries.

Towards the eighteenth century portrait-painters, with few exceptions, lost all sense of individuality, likeness or sincerity. In England the foreigners Lely and Kneller and their followers deliberately conventionalised the art of portraiture, and in their search for what they falsely conceived to be beauty lost all desire for truth. The collection of Court Beauties of the time of Charles II. and William III. at Hampton Court by these two artists illustrates how entirely the power to individualise had been lost. The faces have neither character nor expression. There is an unvarying likeness between them that strikes the observer as false and absurd. So low had the art of portraiture sunk by the middle of the century that the painters, mere hacks, working on purely mechanical lines, earned the contemptuous title of " face-painters." They were indeed craftsmen rather than artists, and craftsmen with little technical skill. Many of these sorry performers were unable to paint anything but the face, and had to employ " drapery men " who made a regular trade of painting in the dress and accessories. Private houses are full of these meaningless portraits, whose only claim to interest is personal to the descendants. So stereotyped had the art of portraiture become, that we can well believe the story of the face-painter who found it so difficult to break with the prevailing custom of painting a gentleman with his hat under his arm that, when required to represent him wearing his hat, he added a second in the orthodox position. These mechanical traditions were at last broken by Hogarth and the great English painters of the eighteenth century, who again raised portraiture to the dignified position of a fine art. The best works of Reynolds and Gainsborough take rank with the greatest portraits of any age. Elegance, refinement and grace of a quality unknown since the days of Van Dyck are their chief characteristics. Above all in their delineation of beautiful women and children do these masters of the classical period of English art stand pre-eminent.

Modern portrait-painting is distinguished by its extraordinary versatility. The names of Millais, Watts, Herkomer, Whistler, Sargent, Fantin-Latour, Carolus-Duran and Lenbach suggest the variety of treatment which has marked the portraiture of the last century. Perhaps the recent development of the science of photography has tended to deprive the mere face-painter of

WHISTLER

PORTRAIT OF HIS MOTHER

Luxembourg, Paris

Manseu photo

his vocation, while enhancing the dignity of the portrait-painter's art.

In looking at portraits it is interesting to note with what infinite variety painters have treated the background. Some have posed their models among the surroundings which belong to them, as Van Eyck painted Arnolfini and his wife standing in their own dwelling-room at Bruges. Holbein shows us *Georg Gisze* the merchant in his counting-house with scales, pen, ink and ledger at his side, and the astronomer *Nicholas Kratzer* with all his scientific instruments about him. In his portrait of *Lord Heathfield* in the National Gallery, Reynolds depicted in the background the Rock of Gibralter lost in the smoke of artillery, in allusion to the memorable siege at which the general had won fame and honour. Sargent poses his women of fashion in the setting of elegant drawing-rooms. Other portrait-painters boldly adopt the simplest backgrounds, either lighter or darker in tone than the face of the model. Velasquez loved to throw up his figures against a luminous atmospheric space ; Rembrandt encircles them in a halo of shadow ; Dürer used a simple brown background slightly darker than the high lights of the face. Holbein when he dispensed with elaboration of detail adopted a plain warm blue or green ; Titian and the Venetians a strong vibrating black, forcing the head into high relief. Some painters of the German School chose backgrounds of decorative tapestry or stencilled design, sometimes inscribing thereon the names of the person represented. With many of the Italians, and after them with Van Dyck and his School, the background became a matter of pure convention and the use of gray marble pillar and red curtain almost a matter of course. From a very early date landscape, either alone or with architecture, was used for a background. Memlinc and his contemporaries painted exquisite little glimpses of country seen through open Gothic windows behind their portraits. Later even landscape backgrounds became conventionalised, and instead of a vista of actual country, Van Dyck, Reynolds and Romney brushed in a mere suggestion of trees and clouds, a scenic effect broadly treated, to give the impression of distance and therefore to enhance that of relief.

GEORG GISZE, MERCHANT OF THE STEELYARD

CHAPTER IX

LANDSCAPE

IT was comparatively late in the history of civilisation
that natural scenery began to be appreciated for its
beauty, and valued by the painter for its pictorial possibilities. The earth must be conquered and subdued
before it can be enjoyed. Not until the Renaissance
did men really become conscious that the world they
lived in was fair to look upon. The longing to gaze
over a wide panorama, which in the fourteenth century
prompted Petrarch to ascend a mountain simply for the
sake of enjoying the view from its summit, is one of the
first symptoms of awakening interest in landscape. So
novel a proceeding suggested nothing short of madness
to his contemporaries. A mountain was to them only
a stronghold against the enemy, or a tiresome obstacle
to communication.

Like portraiture, landscape first appears as an incident
in religious pictures, introduced merely as a decorative
background to set off and relieve the figures, or to
suggest that the scene takes place out of doors. A
straight stem, topped with a few large flatly drawn leaves
for a tree, impossibly shaped rocks against a flat blue
sky, served in early art to suggest a landscape. Such
is the landscape of Giotto's fresco of *Joachim among the
Sheepcotes* at Padua, where the introduction of a flock
of small sheep, somewhat wooden in drawing, emphasises

the pastoral character of the scene.   The same kind of landscape does service in the early frescoes of the Pisan Campo-Santo, and in countless paintings of the Giotteschi.

But before long an advance was made on these primitive, almost symbolical methods.   Masaccio shows himself a pioneer in this as in all other branches of painting. He was the first of the Italians to observe the shapes of mountains and to render the effect of distance.   His frescoes in the Brancacci Chapel in Florence, though injured and faded, proclaim him a master of atmospheric perspective.   The landscape no longer stands up like a wall behind the figures, as in Uccello's diagrammatic *Battle of St. Egidio* in the National Gallery.   But the Florentines were too much interested in the human form to spare any enthusiasm for pure landscape.   According to Leonardo, Botticelli contemptuously averred that a palette of colour thrown against the wall would leave a stain sufficiently defined to represent a landscape. Perugino indeed, for all his Florentine traditions, stands high as a painter of landscape.   His wide expanses of sunlit golden valley give to his pictures that serene, dreamy charm which is their most pleasant quality. He was one of the earliest to realise the beauty of a distant horizon, the depth and spaciousness of the sky, the diffused mellow light of a warm afternoon, characteristics which two centuries later constituted the peculiar charm of Claude and Cuyp.

It was at Venice, however, that landscape-painting developed most rapidly.   Giorgione and Titian treated it with new and fuller appreciation.   In Giorgione's beautiful little *Tempest with Gypsy and Soldier* in Prince Giovanelli's collection, the stormy landscape is fully as important as the small figures, and we find ourselves

GIOTTO

[Arena Chapel, Padua

JOACHIM AMONG THE SHEEPCOTES

wondering whether the landscape was painted for the figures or the figures introduced to enhance the effect of the landscape. Titian's *Noli me tangere* in the National Gallery gives the same impression, and here indeed the figures are the least satisfactory part of the picture. In his great *St. Peter Martyr*, which was destroyed by fire last century, the landscape must have been of consummate beauty. Even Bassano, who with Titian has sometimes been called the father of landscape-painting, because, unlike most of his predecessors, he worked from nature, never painted a landscape without figures and animals. In their treatment of landscape the Italians never forsook that instinct for decorative effect, that insistence upon beauty at all costs, which characterises all their art. Realism in landscape was never their aim, nor would a realistic landscape have been at all in keeping with their ideally beautiful figures.

It was otherwise in the North, where landscape played an important part from the first. The Van Eycks' Ghent altar-piece showed a true appreciation of landscape, and great skill in rendering its features, from the blue mountains of the distance to the flowers that bejewel the grass, and the hedge of roses and vine. The Flemish painters realised too the beautiful effect of a landscape with its sinuous and flowing lines seen through the rigid framework of architecture. We find this contrast in Jan van Eyck's *Madonna* in the Louvre, and Van der Weyden's *Madonna with St. Luke* in Munich. Yet it was a wholly new departure when artists like Patinir, Dürer and Altdorfer set themselves to paint landscape entirely and whole-heartedly for its own sake, aiming at truth to nature rather than at purely decorative effect. Patinir's landscapes indeed are often hard and even unpleasant in colour, as well as grotesque in their primitive, childish drawing of fantastic rocks and mountains. But to him perhaps belongs the honour of being the first to paint an independent landscape. Dürer's water-colour landscapes, which seem to have been sketches made out of doors, testify to an intimate appreciation of natural scenery and true love of colour. Altdorfer's little *Landscape with St. George* in the Munich Gallery shows wonderful freshness, and true delight in the rendering of forest foliage.

But it was not until the seventeenth century that landscape-painting became really important. That century witnessed the rise of two great Schools which were to dominate landscape art for generations to come, the School of so-called Ideal or Classical landscape headed by Claude, and the Naturalistic School, of which the Dutch painters were the pioneers. The rival schools hang side by side in every great collection. There is no mistaking the landscapes of Claude, with their glowing, golden skies and radiant, sunlight effects, their summery atmosphere, their stately pagan architecture. Be their ostensible subject mythological or biblical, *Egeria and her Nymphs*, or *The Marriage of Isaac and Rebecca*, all breathe the same spirit. St. Ursula embarking with her Maidens, or the Queen of Sheba setting forth on her visit to Solomon, mere puppets in a magnificent sea-port, whose waters ripple at the base of lofty classical temples, are only introduced to give a touch of life to the scene, and perhaps a title to the picture. It was under the influence of Italy and Italian skies that Claude's genius developed, an influence which gradually mastered him. To enjoy the studied and formal composition of these idealised landscapes, we must frankly accept them as beautiful and elaborate arrangements, the result of a deliberately chosen point

CLAUDE

THE QUEEN OF SHEBA

of view. That Claude and his followers were incapable of a more literal and realistic rendering of nature were no fair inference. No modern art student could display greater keenness in observation than the great Italianised French master, who spent long days and nights studying the scenery of the Roman Campagna. The distinction is not between what the rival schools could or could not do, but what each wished and set out to do. The atmosphere of Claude's landscape is that of an Italian garden with its straight walks, clipped edges, marble fountains and symmetrical groves, beautiful in its artificiality, but neither challenging nor losing by comparison with the informal beauty of an English lane or wooded upland.

Claude's contemporary, Gaspar Poussin, never quite succeeded in catching his charm, though his landscapes are often grand and impressive. Claude's style found many imitators, who during a century and a half degraded classical landscape by their feeble, tasteless and bombastic productions. Even our own painter Wilson, the English Claude, fell into the error of trying to Italianise every scene he painted. The story is told of how, being commissioned by George III. to paint a picture of Kew Gardens, he sent the king an elaborate classical scene, in which all suggestion of Kew was lost. The very names of Wilson's pictures indicate the classical spirit in which he worked. It has been said of him that he had the fixed idea that the Creator had only made nature to serve as a framework for the Grief of Niobe, and as a vehicle for classical architecture.

Turner was the last and greatest exponent of Claudian tradition. As Hamerton says, he took up Claude's idealism and made it an idealism of his own. He certainly regarded himself as the rival of the earlier master,

as may be seen at the National Gallery, where, in ac-
cordance with the terms of his will, two of his pictures
hang side by side with two by Claude, challenging comparison.   But Turner's range was far wider than that of
the older master, though it never included the intimate
pastoral scenes so typical of English landscape.   It has
been remarked that he never painted an English hedge-
row.   Yet in the Turner room at the National Gallery we
may see him in every one of his many phases, from the
dark heavy seascapes of his youth to such glittering
phantasies of his maturity as *Ulysses deriding Polyphemus*,
Childe Harold's Pilgrimage and *The Bay of Baiae*.

While the classical tradition of landscape was developed in the South by Claude and the Poussins, there
was forming in the North of Europe a school which was
to exercise quite as great an influence on future art.
The Dutch painters, with that strong naturalism which
characterised all their art and unfettered by any traditions of a classical past, set themselves to reproduce the
physical features of their native country.   With Van
Goyen, Hobbema, the Ruysdaels, Cuyp, De Koninck,
William Van der Velde, we find the landscape beauties
of Holland interpreted with exquisite feeling and technical skill, avenues of poplars, wide level plains dotted
with church towers and windmills, quiet silvery canals,
green water-meadows, broad estuaries with shipping,
under many skies, by moonlight or at dawn, in summer
green or winter's snow, as the painters saw them and
felt them, and loved to see and feel them.   Yet for all
their study of nature, Dutch landscape pictures, with
their bronze greens and prevailing brown tones (sometimes the effect, as in Van Goyen's pictures, of the panel
showing through the thin paint), lack that freshness of
green and those lively effects of sparkle and glitter

TURNER

CHILDE HAROLD'S PILGRIMAGE

[*National Gallery*]

JACOB RUYSDAEL.

THE WINDMILL

which the modern landscape artist understands so well.
Some indeed among the Dutchmen, the brothers Both
and Berchem, were Italian and classical rather than
Dutch and naturalistic in intention, deliberately forsak-
ing their native country for Italy and Italian skies.
Again, the pine-clad slopes and wild mountain torrents
of Everdingen and Jacob Ruysdael have a foreign origin.
Everdingen was wrecked on the coast of Norway and
spent some time painting the rugged beauties of that
country, and his pupil Ruysdael, though he had never
been there, frequently painted Norwegian scenery.

In England, landscape in common with other branches
of painting scarcely existed until the eighteenth century, when Wilson and Gainsborough opened the long
series of English landscape-painters. Gainsborough,
upon a foundation of early study of nature and some
acquaintance with Dutch landscape art, built up a
magnificent style of his own, sometimes stately and
decorative, recalling Rubens or Watteau, at others expressing the quiet, intimate charm of English woodland
scenery. But it was in the nineteenth century that
modern landscape art was born. It has indeed been said
that in the province of landscape, the works of the old
masters seem like the exercises of pupils in comparison
with the perfection of modern art. For now to the
faithful rendering of the outward forms of nature is
added an intimate appreciation of her every mood, a
close personal relationship between the artist and his
subject, in complete independence of past tradition.
Constable, the father of this new ideal of landscape art,
declared that whenever he sat down, pencil or brush in
hand, before some chosen scene, his first care was to
forget that he had ever seen any picture. Realising that
the beauty of landscape is largely dependent on the

play of light in sky, on trees and ground, he was the first to render the effect of the glitter and sparkle of sunshine on foliage, the sense of quivering movement in the air and the vivid tones of nature.   Constable's art worked a revolution both in England and France. Directly descended from him are the Barbizon painters, Rousseau, Corot, Daubigny, Diaz, Dupré, the glory of the modern French School.   Living in the heart of the forest of Fontainebleau, each worked out his personal impression of the natural beauties around him.   There is little in common between their work beyond this personal and intimate love of nature.   They painted from no fixed rules, but each, according to his temperament and the mood of the moment, recorded what he saw.   This is the essential characteristic of modern landscape art, this penetrating beyond the outward form to the very soul of nature, as personally revealed to the artist.

Again, in the care and skill with which the painter now seeks to interpret and distinguish the characteristics of time and season, as also in the infinitely greater diversity of the moments of time selected, has modern landscape-painting advanced.   In some of the landscapes of the old masters it is impossible to speak with any certainty as to the season of the year or the hour of day they are intended to suggest.   Until the nineteenth century nearly all landscapes seem to have been painted in the full foliage of late summer.   Winter is only recognisable by the presence of snow and ice.   The tender hues of spring or the brilliant tints of autumn are seldom represented.   Noonday light with its comparative absence of shadows was generally preferred, and it is but seldom that sunrise or sunset effects were attempted.   In modern painting far more is achieved in variety of lighting.   The glare of noon is now justly considered

COROT

LANDSCAPE

[Louvre

Mansell photo]

the worst not the best light for landscape-painting. So much of the beauty of landscape is due to the play of light that by it even the dullest view may be transformed into radiant beauty. The modern painter is often content to rely for his effect upon this alone. All hours of day are now seen to have their special and peculiar beauties and artistic possibilities. Whistler, it has been said, conquered even the night. Modern painting has made night and day, dusk and dawn her own. It is all of a piece with this greater realism that these subtleties of lighting, these fine distinctions of time, should be diligently pursued and faithfully reproduced. The water-colour painters, indeed, from the very nature of their medium, were in this respect in advance of the painters in oil. The speed with which water-colour can be used without long pauses to allow the pigments to dry, as in oil-painting, make it peculiarly suitable for catching fleeting atmospheric effects, momentary beauties of cloud and sunshine.

But apart from the development of landscape-painting, we may further consider other points of view that often suggest themselves in looking at landscape art. The painter may aim at elegance and grace of composition rather than at naturalistic treatment. Claude, indeed, often painted a landscape that never existed, or at least is wholly incapable of identification. Turner, a close observer of nature, took the greatest liberties with his subject, omitting, exaggerating, transposing as he pleased. His sketch of Ben Cruachan in the Highlands is a famous instance of his fearless exaggeration. The outlines of the hills against the sky are not only varied indefinitely from the rather monotonous original, but are raised to the height and dignity of mountains with the same superb assurance. And in this sketch Turner goes even further ; he actually invents a ruined castle on the shore of the lake, a castle in Spain we might say, for it never existed save in his imagination. Sometimes, on the other hand, the painter strives to render the features of the landscape as closely and accurately as possible, as though his object were topographical as well as aesthetic. The artist may indeed chance upon a piece of natural scenery that needs neither arrangement nor modification to form a picture, house or tree, road and bridge being so disposed that they fall directly into the painter's scheme without alteration. But this is not often the case. A landscape usually requires the selective hand of the artist to adapt it to pictorial form. And however closely the painter may keep to his subject, he has his own individual manner of seeing things in landscape as in portraiture, and no two painters will see alike. At the same time, every painter identifies himself more or less with some particular kind of scenery. It may be vast and wide-stretching, the landscape of Rubens, of De Koninck, of Turner, or as with Hobbema, Constable and Corot, small in outlook and intimate. It may be mountainous and terrible, the landscape of Switzerland or Norway, or level and smiling as in England and Holland. But grand scenery is by no means necessarily the most pictorial. Salvator Rosa grappled with its problems, yet often achieved nothing but stupendous pomposity. Turner succeeded with the Alps and Apennines, but, with the exception perhaps of Segantini, no other has dared so much as attempt the superb natural beauties of lofty mountains.

Again in colour, landscape pictures vary, we have seen, from the warm browns of the old masters to the brilliant and tender greens of modern painting. Compare one by an old Dutch painter with its prevailing tones of brown—brown rocks, brown grass, brown trees—with one

Hanfstängl photo]   [Munich

ST. CHRISTOPHER

of the modern French School. In tone and colour the contrast is complete, and no one can doubt which is nearer to nature. These brown tones, often deepened by dark varnishes and changes in the pigments, gave rise in the eighteenth century to a firmly rooted convention of landscape art. The green tints of nature were too often translated into the brown tones of an old Cremona fiddle. No landscape was considered complete without its brown tree in the foreground. When Constable defied these conventions and painted grass and trees green as he saw them, he was taken to task by Sir George Beaumont, the great connoisseur of the day, for having omitted that artistic absurdity the brown tree, and even the painter's explanation that he had painted none because he found none in nature must have sounded to that age something of a splendid paradox. From his time the prevailing brown has given way to the sunlit greens, yellows and pearly grays found in nature herself. The problems of light and *plein air* which engross the modern painter admit of no conventional colouring.

Perhaps in nothing is the skill of the landscape-painter more put to the test than in his rendering of the effects of distance. Foreground, middle distance and background should lead into one another, and carry the eye instinctively and without shock over the whole scene. The early painters found difficulties in these transitions and sometimes ignored them altogether. In so charming a picture as Bouts's *St. Christopher*, the right wing of an altar-piece at Munich, the artist has shown great skill in his rendering of the blue river, its ripples crested with white foam, and of the yellow sunset-sky reflected in the water. He has realised that the distance must not be as clear and bright as the foreground. But he has not been able to modulate, and

G

there is no real middle distance.   The brown rocks in the
forefront of the picture meet the blue rocks in the background, and the water fades abruptly without transition.
There is a peculiar charm in a landscape that carries the
eye into unmeasured distances, where all definition of
form is merged in mysterious haze.   It is the charm of
Perugino, of Claude and of Turner, whose pictures
satisfy and delight the eye with this feeling for infinite
space.

We often notice when looking at a landscape-painting
how artfully the painter has contrived that the lines of
the background emphasise and repeat those of the
figures, trees and buildings of the foreground, bringing
them together and making for unity of effect.   Even
where the lines are not actually repeated, foreground and
background must be related to one another either by
likeness or effective contrast.   Painters like Cuyp and
Troyon perfectly understood this necessity, and when
they painted their favourite cattle large and prominent
in the foreground they would insure a wide and spacious
view in one part of the landscape to give the proper
sense of space and absence of restraint.   The effect is
often enhanced by the use of a low, level horizon.

Almost all painters have realised the value of introducing figures in their landscape scenes.   Indeed, as we
have seen, at one time the figures, however small and
inconspicuous, gave a pretext for the landscape, and often
furnished a name for the picture.   Entire absence of life
in a landscape is comparatively rare.   Even a flight of
birds in the sky suggests some movement to relieve the
passivity of nature, which without a sign of life is apt to
be monotonous in art as well as in reality.   Sometimes it
happens that the landscape-painter has little or no skill
in drawing figures.   Turner's are sometimes woefully

CONSTABLE

THE HAY-WAIN

clumsy and inadequate to their magnificent setting. We know that among the Dutch painters it was a recognised practice to employ a skilled figure-painter to supplement the deficiencies of the landscape artists. Such a division of labour would be impossible in a modern impressionist landscape, where the figures form an integral part of the whole scheme and are not merely introduced to give it life. In much the same way the presence of some building, farmhouse or windmill, helps to express the true proportion of the scene as well as to add an element of human interest for which the fairest landscape ever conceived may be the richer. Many great landscape-painters have introduced architecture into their pictures, be it the woodland cottage of Hobbema, the farms and homesteads of Constable, the stately classical piles of Claude or the fantastic palaces of Turner.

Beyond this many painters have made architecture their subject to the exclusion of all else. The pictorial effect of architecture pure and simple may be appreciated in the Italian scenes of Canaletto and Guardi, in the ruined temples of Robert, in the church and street views of the Dutch masters Berckheyde, Van der Heyden, Peter Neefs and De Witte in the seventeenth century, and of Bosboom in our own day. Canaletto and Guardi's Venetian street and canal scenes have not only pictorial but archaeological interest, as recording the appearance of famous buildings, many of which are now swept away. Canaletto excelled in elaborate composition and accurate perspective. To his pupil Guardi we look rather for charm of colour and atmospheric effects. Of the Dutch architectural painters some devoted themselves to street scenes and the exterior of churches and houses, often with the added charm of a waterway flanked by avenues of trees.   Others delighted in spacious church-interiors which afforded equal scope for fine perspective and delicate treatment of light and colour.   In our own country David Roberts and Prout are pre-eminently distinguished as painters of architecture.

Reference has already been made to the painting of the sky in landscape pictures.   The first step was the substitution of a blue sky graduated to the horizon for the gold backgrounds in common use until the fourteenth century and even later.   The painting of sky and clouds is indeed a vital part of landscape art.   Do the heavens frown or smile?   Are they placid, or is there a sense of wind or at least of fresh air?   Is the sky transparent, light-reflecting, neither papery, heavy nor opaque?   Do the clouds float, suspended as it were in the blue, or sail majestically by with proper sense of pomp and circumstance?   Has the painter fully rendered their very texture, making them neither woolly nor wooden, nor lacking the fullness of form by which they bulk large in the sky, conferring dignity upon the whole scene?   Compare the heavy marbled clouds of Patinir with the luminous silvery skies of Teniers.   The superb effects of clear, rain-washed skies, throwing into stronger relief the black passing thunder-cloud, were especially beloved by Ruysdael and Constable; while for a bright, transparent firmament stretching cloudlessly into infinite regions of azure space Claude has never been surpassed. The part played by the sky in a landscape is more or less important, according as the line of horizon be low or, as in many modern pictures, so high that but a narrow band is seen above it.   A low horizon gives greater space and distance, and affords scope for interesting and varied sky effects.

Marine painting or seascape must be considered as a

branch of landscape art. It developed side by side with landscape-painting proper. It is but seldom that we find the sea introduced into early pictures even into the background, though lakes and rivers are of frequent occurrence. There is indeed a little picture in the National Gallery by Niccolò da Foligno with a view of the sea in the distance. But it was in Holland that marine painting first began to play an important part, for the sea was both the glory and the menace of this low-lying naval power. What more natural than that a school of sea painters should arise under Van Goyen, De Vlieger, William Van der Velde and Van der Cappelle? They painted placid coast-scenes for the most part, fishing boats and ships of war at anchor, with strong feeling for light and reflections upon the smooth surface of water. Backhuizen delighted in storms and shipwrecks, risking his life in an open boat to study the effects of lofty waves and perilous seas. Turner's early sea-pieces, the *Shipwreck*, *Calais Pier* and *Fishing Boats in a Breeze*, exhibit much the same spirit, while in his quiet harbour scenes and waterways flooded with golden light, painted in rivalry with Claude, it is the placid beauty of deep, still water on which he dwells. Since Turner's time the sea has been painted in all its many moods. Courbet in his *Wave* in the Louvre has rendered the overwhelming power and majestic curves of a single great rolling breaker. Mesdag and Henry Moore delight in expanses of ocean, with or without hint of land. The Cornish artists paint the sea from the shore. Indeed modern marine painting, like modern landscape, knows no limit to what it dares attempt.

CHAPTER X

GENRE

GENRE pictures form the last of our three groups. The development of modern painting has certainly rendered them the most numerous, and perhaps the most popular class, though from their very nature they occupy a less elevated position in the art of painting. The term Genre is used loosely enough to cover a multitude of pictures and artistic sins. It extends over so wide a field because the term is used not only in reference to the actual subject, but to the manner in which the picture is treated. From the point of view of subject merely genre-painting includes all those pictures which do not attempt to represent special individuals or particular incidents, but types of people and ordinary events, such as are of continual and perhaps daily occurrence in actual life. The subjects depicted are common rather than uncommon, trivial rather than important. A soldier handing a dispatch to his officer, a child playing with its doll, a group of men carousing at an inn, a number of schoolboys engaged in snow-balling, a woman puzzling over a love letter are all typically genre subjects. Again, pictures of so-called still life, arrangements of household utensils, flower and fruit pieces, may be conveniently grouped under this head. With Genre, too, animal-painting must be considered. Thus from the point of view of subject,

genre pictures will depict homely scenes and events,
tell merry or sad stories, illustrate passages from books
or plays, point a moral or perpetuate a joke, in fact be
either domestic, anecdotal, literary, dramatic or merely
fanciful.

On the other hand, pictures which at first sight and
from the point of view of their subject alone would
appear to belong to some other class may be considered
as genre on account of the spirit in which they are
treated. A purely religious or historical subject may
be painted in such a homely matter-of-fact way, that it
almost becomes a genre picture. This genre manner of
painting may be found long before a purely genre subject was ever thrown upon a canvas. In its early days
painting was too serious a business, with too many
important tasks to accomplish, to busy itself with subjects so trivial as a child's grief over a broken jug or the
bargainings of a vendor of herrings. Thus the beginnings of genre-painting must be sought in the minor
incidents in the religious pictures of early art, in the
frescoes and altar-pieces of Florentine painters like Ghirlandaio and Andrea del Sarto, of the Venetians Crivelli,
Carpaccio and Bassano. How homely and intimate is
Ghirlandaio's treatment of the *Death of S. Fina* in the
beautiful fresco at S. Gimignano. In Crivelli's *Annunciation* in the National Gallery, the little bed-chamber of
the Virgin, with its shelves over the bed stocked with
bottles, plates and books, inevitably suggests the genre-
painting of a later date, when these accessories would
have been in themselves sufficient material for a picture.
In his *Dream of St. Ursula* in the Venice Academy,
Carpaccio shows the same interest in the everyday
domestic side of life, treating it with perfect simplicity
and candour, quite in the genre manner. We are less

surprised to find touches of genre in the more homely religious pictures of the northern painters. In an early German rendering of the Birth of the Virgin in the Munich Gallery, the domestic details of the scene have been elaborated with peculiar zest. The careful German housewife is giving out the linen from a well-stocked chest, two nurses superintend the child's bath, testing its temperature, while a maid pours in boiling water from a saucepan.

But it was in the seventeenth century that genre first became a really independent branch of painting. Pure genre was the particular contribution of the painters of the Netherlands. A homely people delighted in homely subjects. A somewhat phlegmatic and material race knew no craving for the mystical or the obscure, demanded no works of high religious significance, indeed their strict Calvinistic tenets permitted none. Their houses were small and their pictures must be small accordingly. The wealthy *bourgeoisie* of Holland delighted in that genre style of painting which has been well described as the very *bourgeoisie* of art. The Netherlands was indeed the land of genre-painting at its highest. Rembrandt treated religious scenes in a purely genre manner. Van Ostade, Brouwer, Terburg, Metzu, Jan Steen, Gerard Dou, Peter Breughel, Teniers, and a hundred other artists of their time, were all strictly genre-painters, whose like the world has never seen again. Van Ostade and Brouwer painted the dark interiors of taverns, peopled by drinking, brawling boers, and rendered them with incomparable vigour and realism. Teniers treated indoor and outdoor scenes of daily life with equal mastery. Terburg and Metzu loved rather the sumptuous splendours and substantial luxury of elegant domesticity in their own more civilised surroundings. Jan

Steen excels by his perennial gaiety and frank pleasure-loving moods. Dou delighted in marvellously delicate finish and harmonious colouring. Nicolas Maes touches the tender and pathetic chord of human life, but it is true sentiment not false sentimentality with which he makes his appeal. Vermeer and De Hoogh revel in effects of sunlight flooding parlour or paved courtyard. But in the case of all these masters of genre, Jan Steen perhaps excepted, it is useless to look for any great individuality of expression or characterisation. They did not attempt to give it or value it if found. They painted ordinary men in ordinary situations, not heroes in a moment of crisis. Their subjects were those which spoke most directly to the spectator. They demanded no knowledge of history or archaeology, no religious belief, no book-learning. They appealed to the common man and woman with intimate confidence, and they did not appeal in vain. George Eliot has emphasised this power of the Dutch masters in a familiar passage: " It is for this rare, precious quality of truthfulness that I delight in many Dutch paintings which lofty-minded people despise. I find a source of delicious sympathy in these faithful pictures of a monotonous, homely existence which has been the fate of so many more of my fellow-mortals than a life of pomp or of absolute indigence, of tragic suffering or of world-stirring actions. I turn without shrinking from cloud-borne angels, from prophets, sibyls and heroic warriors to an old woman bending over her flower-pot or eating her solitary dinner, while the noonday light, softened perhaps by a screen of leaves, falls on her mob-cap and just touches the rim of her spinning wheel and her stone jug, and all those cheap common things which are the precious necessaries of life to her."

The example thus given in Holland spread throughout Europe, and every country where painting has
flourished has her genre-painters of note. Italy produced Longhi, the Hogarth of the South, a master of
real merit. Standing entirely alone and by far the
greatest of French genre-painters is Chardin, whose
quiet restful art seems almost out of touch with the artificiality of the eighteenth century. His *Grace before
Meat* and *Mère laborieuse* in the Louvre show him the
equal of even the greatest of the Dutchmen. How
mawkish and shallow appears the meretricious Greuze
by the side of Chardin's dignified simplicity and re-
ticence. But this period in France was dominated by a
style of genre as different in character from that of
Holland as is the Gallic temperament from the Dutch.
Watteau, Lancret and Fragonard painted no ruddy-
faced women in homely garments, occupied with culinary
and domestic pursuits, no elaborate green-grocers' or
poulterers' shops, but in their place elegantly dressed
ladies and gentlemen of the Court, dancing elaborate
minuets in satin shoes or feasting from exquisite china
upon the greensward of some aristocratic château. If
this be genre it is idyllic genre. As different again and
more nearly allied to the genre of Holland is the style
of Meissonier, "the Dutch little master," as his friends
called him. Although in colour he cannot compare with
the best of the Dutch painters, Terburg and Metzu, in
minute delicacy of execution he is scarcely inferior. In
Spain Murillo, the contemporary of the Dutch masters,
brought genre into fashion with his peasant boys and
street arabs, broadly and vigorously handled. Even
Velasquez in his salad days produced *Bodegones* or
kitchen scenes, an *Old Woman cooking Eggs* and *Two
Young Men at a Meal.* Goya's genre was either diabolic

in character or else painted in the elegant style of the contemporary French School. Modern genre-painting in Spain is represented by the fashionable Fortuny, a painter of specious brillance and true southern love of colour and display.

English genre-painting begins with Hogarth, who treated art in the didactic spirit of the moral reformer. With a painter of less splendid genius this standpoint would inevitably have spelt ruin to his art ; but Hogarth was an artist before he became a reformer, and his fine series of *Marriage à la Mode* and *The Rake's Progress* are far from being mere sermons in paint. Hogarth's mantle fell upon Wilkie, who, however, painted without the earlier artist's didactic intention. Wilkie, the Scottish Teniers, as he has been called, consciously sat at the feet of his great Dutch and Flemish predecessors, and often painted with a work of Teniers or Van Ostade on an easel beside him. A glance at his pictures *The Blind Fiddler* and *The Village Festival* reveals how much he owed to earlier masters. The tendency of English genre in the direction of story-telling is here already strongly marked. The history of nineteenth-century art in this country is largely the history of its genre-painters, of whom we can merely mention Mulready, Leslie, Frith, Orchardson and Alma Tadema.

Judging from the annual exhibitions of modern paint-ing in London, Paris, Munich and Vienna, it would appear that genre is the most popular art of the day. In England at least it holds almost undisputed sway, especially in the form of anecdotal or literary genre in its feeblest and most sentimental aspect. Pictures of this class are produced in their thousands by painters of little or no artistic power, who seek to atone by the obvious prettiness of the incident for deficiency of skill and commonplace rendering. The best genre-painters never stoop to this device. The greatest care nothing whether they paint a pretty scene or not, since of any they can make a beautiful picture. For in genre-painting, as we have already seen, the subject is of less importance than the manner in which it is treated. This is especially the case in pictures of still life. There may be but little to interest or please the unseeing eye in a group of common household utensils and fruit placed together upon a table ; but of these unpromising materials true artists like Chardin and the Dutchmen De Heem, Heda or Kalf will by skilful arrangement, by bringing out unobserved subtleties of light and colour, by heightened contrasts and harmonious composition, produce a true work of art. The painter of *natures mortes* requires but the simplest materials, a few copper or brass pots and pans, a loaf of bread, a piece of raw meat, some pewter or earthenware kitchen utensils, with fruit or vegetables. Such subjects are naturally most effective when treated on a small scale. Vast canvases of dead game and fruit, such as those of Snyders, can scarcely fail of monotony, the very insignificance of the subject falling far short of the heroic proportions of its representation. Their merit lies almost exclusively in their brilliant technical qualities. A still-life picture should be like a jewel burning and glowing with colour and reflected light.

In flower-painting, the materials, instead of being the humblest and simplest, are the most beautiful and complex. Here too the artist's powers of selection and arrangement will be called into play. In the faithful rendering of the form and texture of blossom and leaf the Flemish artists Jan Breughel and Seghers are unsurpassed. Yet the stiff grouping and cold, hard colour often rob their pictures of real charm and naturalism. In seizing upon the essential beauties of natural forms, in freer and less studied arrangements of foliage, in lighter and more graceful rendering, European flower-painters have been left far behind by the artists of Japan.

Finally a word must be found for a class of painters who have chosen to devote themselves to the painting of animals. As might be expected in a land of pastures, many of the Dutch artists excelled in the painting of cattle. Pre-eminent among them are Cuyp, Paul Potter, Adrian Van der Velde, Karel du Jardin and Weenix, while Hondecoeter has no rival in the poultry-yard. Rubens and Snyders in Flanders are noted for their vigorous representation of animals in motion. In our own time animal-painting has become an important and independent branch of art. In France the names of Courbet, Troyon and Rosa Bonheur, in England those of Morland, Landseer, Briton-Riviere and Swan readily suggest themselves. The animal-painter must render the characteristic movements and attitudes of the brute beast, as well as the texture of skin or fur. Above all he must catch the true animal expression and not fall into Landseer's error of giving a sentimental, almost human look to his dogs and horses. The scope of the animal-painter has been greatly extended by travel and photography since the days when Dürer drew and engraved his famous rhinoceros from hearsay and the slight pencil drawing made by an eye-witness of this quite unfamiliar animal.

CHAPTER XI

DRAWING

THE simplest and most obvious method of representation in pictorial art is by the use of outline. To
test this we have only to look at some example of early
painting, in which light and shade and atmospheric effects
are either entirely wanting or are still so elementary
and subordinate that they scarcely play any part in
the whole. The childhood of art is represented by the
prehistoric cave-dweller scratching in outline upon the
rock with a sharp flint the familiar forms of reindeer and
mammoth. These early beginnings may be likened to
the first efforts of a child drawing figures of men and
horses in the simplest and most conventional outlines.
It is a further step when these boundary lines are filled
in with flat washes of colour, a stage corresponding to
the beginnings of the art of painting. Originally the
graphic arts concerned themselves with two dimensions
only, length and breadth, and outline was quite able to
express these. Even when the representation of a third
dimension, depth, came to be insisted on, outline still
played an important part in producing, by means of
linear perspective, the effect of solidity.

In speaking of drawing, the word is of course not used
here in its limited sense of representation in a particular
medium, pen, pencil or charcoal, but in its broader sense
as a means of expressing form. It is convenient for the

moment to consider the actual drawing of a picture apart from its colour or light and shade, for, however intimately they are bound up together in theory, in practice we are perfectly clear of our meaning when we speak of the drawing of a picture being good or bad, accurate or careless. It is impossible indeed actually to separate form from colour, since in painting form is expressed in terms of colour. Yet if its colour be eliminated, as in a photograph, the drawing of the picture will be laid bare. A painter may be a good colourist and at the same time a bad draughtsman, or on the other hand he may spoil a finely drawn design by crude, disagreeable colouring. It is the greatest masters who unite a fine sense of form with a strong instinct for colour. Drawing is indeed the foundation of pictorial art, from its early days of carving a rude figure on a stone to the perfect mastery over the most intricate forms which we find in modern art.

By the term drawing we mean more than the mere rendering of the outline of objects, a man or a mountain silhouetted against the sky. Drawing includes the definition of every detail of form within those boundary lines, the rendering of the shape of every feature, of the hair, of the draperies, of every rock and tree. It covers the painter's feeling for the shapes of things, their solidity, their roundness or squareness, the way they bulk before him, even their character so far as this depends upon their shape.

The use of outline to define form is one of the conventions of the painter's art. It is true that in nature no such thing as a line exists. Forms melt into each other by imperceptible gradations. Indeed it has often been contended that in pictorial art drawing is nothing but the result of differences of colour, and that lines are

merely successions of points at which coloured surfaces
meet.   The end of one colour, said Leonardo, is only the
beginning of another, and ought not to be called a line.
Theoretically speaking, this is true, and mature art at
least both sees and draws in masses of colour and light
and shade rather than in lines.   If we examine a picture
by Rembrandt, Velasquez, Reynolds or Turner, we find
no lines separating one form from another.   The shapes
of things are defined by patches of colour, not harshly
juxtaposed, but with their edges broken or blurred.   Art
can, of course, reproduce nature only by means of some
convention, and a well-defined outline is the most obvious
means of indicating form.   In early Italian art the actual
drawing of the picture was of first importance, colour
being used almost as an afterthought in a flat, conventional manner, to fill in the outlines.   Indeed the Florentine painters never freed themselves from a certain
hardness of line.   Before beginning to paint a picture,
it was usual for them to draw on the prepared ground,
often with pen and ink, every detail of figures, draperies,
background and ornament.   In such pictures as Filippo
Lippi's *Annunciation* and Botticelli's *Mars and Venus*,
both in the National Gallery, this hard, firm outline may
easily be seen.   The profile portraits of Verrocchio and
other Florentine painters are tightly confined within
sharply cut outlines, silhouetted against a dark background, producing an effect of comparative flatness.
Many of Holbein's portraits show the same characteristic.
If he can relieve his flesh colour against the dark mass of
the sitter's hair or hat he is content, but where it falls
against a light background he is not above emphasising
the form by a strongly-defined black line.   The colouring
of the picture is simple, and plays, as compared with the
drawing, especially of the features, but a minor part;

PORTRAIT OF A LADY

indeed we have only to compare a painting by this master with one of his chalk-drawings to understand how little is due to the colour. Compare these with pictures by Titian, Correggio, Veronese, Rubens and Rembrandt, where we scarcely ever find strong outlines. Indeed where they do occur, as, for instance, in the figure of the Madonna in Titian's *Assumption*, they are the work of the restorer and not of the master. Colours blend into one another instead of being sharply separated and inclosed within boundary lines. In either case a particular aspect of beauty is obtained.

Many pictures owe their permanent value in art and their chief charm in our eyes to the peculiar feeling for line which the artist possessed, and to his skill and facility in draughtsmanship, just as others please by richness or harmony of colour, or the delicacy of their effects of light and shade. It has been said that every special virtue a painting may possess is relative to its other virtues. Such pictures as Mantegna's *Triumph of Julius Caesar* at Hampton Court and Signorelli's *Pan* in the Berlin Museum charm the eye in the first instance by their wonderful feeling for line. Botticelli's *Pallas and Centaur* in the Pitti and his *Calumny* in the Uffizi, with their delicate, sinuous curves, appeal in the same manner. Ingres's *La Source* in the Louvre shows great sensitiveness to the subtle lines of the nude figure, though even its warmest admirers cannot approve his hard colour and expressionless features. David's reclining figure of *Madame Récamier* shows exquisite beauty of line, and many of Leighton's and Burne-Jones's pictures, claim and win our admiration by the same quality.

Drawing is one of the first points of view from which a picture is usually regarded, and therefore one of the earliest to be criticised. We are all so familiar with the

H

forms of natural objects, and especially of the human figure, that a grave error in their representation strikes us at once, though trifling faults of detail are often over-looked. It is far otherwise with colour, and still more so with light and shade. The most flagrant incongruities of colour and tone go unnoticed because the eye of the spectator is not trained to perceive them. In a picture representing a nude figure there would be ten critics to notice that the drawing of the shoulder or leg was care-less or incorrect for one who would observe the faults in the colouring of the flesh or falseness of tone. While, therefore, many painters are distinguished by the excel-lence of their draughtsmanship, there are others who, whatever merits they may possess as colourists or chiar-oscurists, fail sometimes conspicuously in this respect. Their figures seem to stand shakily, as if a push would upset them. The feet, though touching the ground, do not rest upon it. The limbs appear puffy and clumsy. In early painting inexperience and lack of knowledge account for much. In other cases, even in comparatively modern times, want of training and inadequate study of the human figure are sufficient explanation.

Sometimes indeed it happens that good draughtsmen deliberately sacrifice absolute correctness of drawing in quest of elements of beauty that appeal more forcibly to them, as where to gain decorative effect or dignity and grandeur the painter exaggerates the height of a figure, or uses his artist's licence to bring its lines into harmony with his design. This is especially the case with painters pre-eminent for their strong feeling for beauty of line. Botticelli has already been mentioned as illustrating this feeling. But his long, slender figures in the *Allegory of Spring* are physically impossible, though no one would question their fine decorative qualities. He used the

GIORGIONE

SLEEPING VENUS

[Dresden]

Hanfstängl photo]

human figure as so much pattern from which to weave his designs, disregarding structural possibility. So, too, the drawing of Giorgione's *Sleeping Venus* in Dresden is perhaps not absolutely correct. The right foot should be visible, though as its appearance would break the exquisitely flowing and sinuous lines of the reclining figure, which again harmonise with and repeat the gently rising mountain slopes behind, the painter has deliberately suppressed it.

But it is to inexperience, lack of knowledge or carelessness that inadequate draughtmanship must generally be attributed. No one can be surprised to find faults and weaknesses of drawing in early painting. To the primitive masters the drawing of certain parts of the human figure, especially the hands and feet, presented almost insuperable difficulties. They scarcely ever succeeded in making them anything but wooden and lifeless in appearance. Claw-like extremities or stiff angular fingers are painfully common until comparatively late in Italian art. The drawing of the feet is still more peculiar. This was, of course, due partly to ignorance of anatomy and perspective, partly to tradition. As time went on, the substitution of the living model for the almost symbolic treatment which had gone before, and an acquaintance with the laws of perspective and anatomy, brought greater sureness and accuracy of draughtsmanship.

In our day painters receive in the life-school so thorough a grounding that faulty drawing is unusual. Modern draughtsmanship is generally fluent and facile, if not always close and searching. Shaky figures and boneless, invertebrate forms which do not really stand upon their legs are scarcely the faults of this generation. The modern artist who has had a good training has hardly to think of his drawing as a difficulty to be overcome, though a subtle and refined instinct for form is always confined to the greatest. The problems of the proportions of the figure, the relative size of head, trunk and limbs, problems which Leonardo and Dürer worked out experimentally with elaborate diagrams and formulae, have become the mere rudiments of the painter's art. Even the difficulties of representing men or animals in motion are no longer as great as before. The observations made by instantaneous photography have contributed largely to greater accuracy, though not necessarily to greater beauty. For instance, we now know exactly how the legs of a horse actually move according to the gait or speed of the moment, and accuracy on so comparatively trivial a matter is not unnaturally insisted upon when there is no longer any excuse for error.

The drawing of the human figure must necessarily depend to a considerable extent on a knowledge of anatomy. To the artist anatomy has often been a fetish; to the layman it has as often proved a bugbear. The explanation would seem to be that anatomy, like perspective, is to be regarded as an aid to correct and beautiful drawing, and not as an end in itself. When Antonio Pollaiuolo, one of the first enthusiasts for the science, painted his great *St. Sebastian* in the National Gallery, he not unnaturally laid undue emphasis on the muscular construction of the figures, purposely representing them in every attitude of violent strain. The secrets of anatomy were then in the nature of discoveries, and as a pioneer the painter desired to display his laboriously acquired knowledge. Michelangelo's intimate familiarity with the human figure as a sculptor showed itself strongly in his painting, and this sculptor-painter's figures, whether nude or draped, invariably suggest a wholly ideal state of physical development and muscu-

larity, which in his hands alone escaped exaggeration
and brutality.   His prophets, sibyls and youths on the
ceiling of the Sistine Chapel, brawny, massive, colossal,
inspire only awe, and convey the idea of marvellous,
restrained power.   His followers, Daniele da Volterra
and his like, copied and exaggerated this muscularity
and colossal treatment, but wholly failed to realise the
inherent majesty and grand self-composure of Michelangelo's nudes.

The German and Dutch painters rarely attempted the
nude, completely concealing the form under heavy draperies.   Yet even in such cases some knowledge of the
structure of the human form is essential.   Although the
body is entirely covered by drapery, the spectator should
be conscious of its presence underneath.   A finely drawn
figure, however elaborately draped, must be as carefully
constructed as a nude ; indeed many painters make nude
studies of all their figures, adding the draperies afterwards.   The draughtsman must indicate the roundness
of the arm under the sleeve, the position of the limbs
under the draperies.   It is all the difference between the
living form and the lay figure.   In this some of our great
painters, Reynolds and Romney, occasionally failed.
Reynolds's well-known ignorance of anatomy, which none
regretted more bitterly than the painter himself, was no
doubt largely responsible for his indifferent modelling of
hands and limbs.

The treatment of draperies in all their infinite variety
is in itself a test of good draughtsmanship.   Draperies
may add dignity to the figure or emphasise the sense of
movement ; they may be simple or elaborate, broadly
rendered or broken into minute folds.   Compare the vol-
uminous fretted folds in pictures of the Flemish painters
or of Lucas van Leyden and Dürer, with the broad simple

masses used by the Venetians, or the slight, clinging draperies of Leighton and Albert Moore, which suggest every line and curve of the figure beneath.

The question of linear perspective, so important an element of drawing, demands rather fuller mention. Even the untrained eye is quick to observe any flagrant faults of perspective in a picture. Linear perspective is the means by which the appearance of solid objects and their relative distance from the eye can be rendered on a flat surface. Drawing is itself a convention, by which objects of three dimensions, height, breadth and depth, are represented on a surface of two only, height and breadth. The third dimension, depth, is indicated by means of perspective. Perspective is both natural and scientific, a matter of eye and a matter of mathematical rules and formulae. Before the discovery of its laws in the fifteenth century, painters had to trust entirely to the eye. Sometimes their perspective was correct, almost as it were by accident, but really owing to their careful copying of nature; more often it was grotesquely incorrect and impossible, and this fact gives primitive pictures much of their quaintness and lack of reality. The ground seems to stand up as a solid wall; the roofs slope at impossible angles; parallel lines fail to converge. The point of sight being often too high, we seem to look down into the picture, while the architecture seems to topple forward; or, in the case of an interior, the room slopes up, and objects on a table look as though they were slipping off it. In the pictures of Giotto and his School the architecture is absurdly out of proportion to the size of the figures. These unfortunate giants could never inhabit the pigmy houses provided for them. The Florentine painter Uccello was one of the first who, obviously dissatisfied with the results of trusting to correctness of eye alone, set himself to work out the principles of perspective. Just as some of his contemporaries became enthusiastic students of the science of anatomy, so he sought to discover the key to the mysteries of "that beautiful thing Perspective." His *Battle of St. Egidio* in the National Gallery shows the result of his studies, and illustrates both the problems and the difficulties of the science. But nothing can be further from reality than the result achieved by this pursuit of scientific realism. Again, the difficulty of representing a recumbent figure, seen end-on, by means of foreshortening baffled the worthy Uccello for all his devoted study. We have only to compare his fallen soldier depicted thus in this picture with Mantegna's *Dead Christ* in the Brera to appreciate the later artist's triumph over the difficulty. In his mastery over perspective and foreshortening Mantegna was rivalled only by his successor Correggio, whose painted cupola in the Cathedral at Parma is a *tour de force*. So far is the illusion carried by means of violent foreshortening that it is almost as though the roof were lifted off, and we could look above and beyond it into a sky peopled with flying figures.

Some of the greatest masters of design have deliberately transgressed the rigid laws of perspective. Even Raphael did not consider himself strictly bound to observe them when a particular effect was at stake, and it has often been pointed out that in his *School of Athens* in the Vatican there are two vanishing points, one for the architecture, another for the figures. The same criticism is made of Veronese's *Marriage of Cana*, in which also the capitals of the Doric columns are extraordinarily incorrect. A more modern instance of glaringly false perspective is the ceiling in one of Hogarth's engravings in the series of *The Idle Apprentice*. In point of fact no painter works with these scientific principles consciously before him. They are in the background of his mind, and, relying on his trained eye, he draws with just sufficient correctness of perspective for his purpose. Consequently, if we apply the principles of perspective in all their mathematical rigidity, many pictures which perfectly satisfy the eye will be found wanting. As Ruskin said of Turner, who was Professor of Perspective at the Royal Academy, he did not even know what he professed, and probably never drew a single building in true perspective in his life ; he drew them only with as much perspective as suited him.

CHAPTER XII

COLOUR

WHEN looking at pictures it is not generally their colour that first attracts the ordinary spectator's interest. His attention is turned to the significance of the subject and the drawing of the picture before he seriously observes its colour. The reason may be found largely in the difficulty and resulting want of confidence in understanding it. Questions of colour seem so technical, so scientific in comparison with other considerations. We do not feel that we can evolve a perfectly satisfactory theory or explanation of them out of our inner consciousness. We may like or dislike the colouring of any particular picture, we may condemn it as impossible, or praise it for its brilliance, but it is with a half uneasy feeling which shrinks from cross-examination and avoids particulars or analysis. And yet colour is of the very essence of painting. We have seen that, theoretically speaking, it includes form, and is therefore the basis of drawing. In the same way, as we shall see, it is inseparably bound up with chiaroscuro or light and shade.

There is no need to do more than touch upon the scientific or physiological side of the question of colour in considering it as one of the chief elements of beauty and interest in a picture. It will be enough to start with the familiar fact that colours are the result of rays of white light falling upon various substances or pigments, each of which has the property of absorbing some of these rays and reflecting others.   Thus red paint absorbs all other rays except red ones, which it reflects ; violet absorbs all except violet rays, and so on.   But in practice the effect is infinitely more complicated, because no substance can ever be completely isolated, and each gives not only its own peculiar red or green or violet rays, but also reflections from all adjoining substances. Further, each colour has its contrasting or complementary colour, green being the complementary of red, orange of blue and yellow of violet.   Thus after looking intently for a few moments at a patch of red on a white ground, the eye sees more or less distinctly that the red patch is surrounded by an aureole of its complementary, and on turning immediately to a plain white ground a patch of green is distinctly visible, an experiment familiar through the popular advertisement of Pears' Soap.

Again, where there are two colours side by side, each surrounded by its complementary, these complementary colours will, by mixing where they meet or overlap, again produce a new combination.   We have said that the eye sees these complementary colours more or less distinctly, because their distinctness actually depends on the presence of a white ground on which alone the complementary colour can be clearly perceived, and even then only after somewhat prolonged fixing of the eye.

Another simple effect of the laws of optics concerns the spectator as much as the painter.   When going round a gallery with notebook or catalogue, the colouring of the pictures will appear more brilliant from the fact of continually looking up from the white paper. There are two further elementary laws to be borne in mind, that complementary colours when placed side by side heighten one another, while colours which are not complementary placed side by side diminish one another. Thus blue placed by the side of its complementary orange appears more intensely blue because it receives the addition of the blue which is the complementary of orange.

These few laws are mentioned here only to emphasise the complexity of the problems that meet the colourist. As stated in the form of scientific principles they are comparatively modern discoveries, almost of our own time ; but their practical importance was fully realized centuries before, and Giorgione, Veronese and Rubens obeyed them none the less implicitly that they had not yet been formulated. Nor must it be thought that the artist of the present day paints his pictures by the light of these rules. For him they are largely negative ; he knows that if he paints a red skirt below a blue bodice the brilliance of both colours will be diminished, while a green field will appear less green against a blue sky. These same principles are unconsciously respected by every woman who chooses the colour of her dress with reference to her complexion. As Eastlake pointed out, " Flesh is never more glowing than when compared with red, never ruddier than in the neighbourhood of green, never fairer than when contrasted with black, nor richer or deeper than when opposed to white."

Since the beginning of painting in the Middle Ages the use of colour has advanced through many stages, from the simple conventional colouring of the early fresco-painter to the highly elaborated and realistic treatment of our own day. Go in the National Gallery from the Florentine room to the Venetian, from the Venetian to the Dutch, the Spanish or the English. What different colour-impressions we get from each ; gay, glowing, sombre or cold. Leaving all other considerations out of

sight, compare from this point of view of colour alone
pictures by Fra Angelico, Titian, Rembrandt, Hogarth
and Claude Monet.   Wherein lies the difference between
these painters ? Partly, perhaps, in the different colours
they used, but chiefly in the manner in which they used
them.

Primitive painters like Fra Angelico worked with few
colours, keeping each distinct from the other.   In painting a blue robe they would use paler blue for the high
lights and a deeper blue for the shadows, regardless of the
surrounding colours with their reflections and counter-
effects.   They relied almost entirely upon flat surfaces of
simple colour, often in sharp, even crude contrast, with few
shadows and few dark tones.   Their colours are generally
wonderfully transparent and pure, the masses pleasantly
disposed ; but for all their charm we cannot help feeling
that here colouring is expressed in far simpler fashion than
can be found in nature. The sky is of a uniform blue, behind
brown rocks and dark green trees, whose foliage is often
defined with touches of gold.   Figures in bright green,
crimson, blue or purple dresses, sometimes shot with gold,
wearing richly gilded halos and ornaments, are grouped
in more or less formal arrangement.   The frequent use
of gold in itself gives an appearance of unreality.   The
effect may be pleasing, though wholly unlike nature.
But it was as near nature as the artists could approach.
We cannot believe that Fra Angelico or Memlinc were
deliberately and of set purpose simplifying the complex
shades and tints of nature, as is often done by the
decorative painters of our own day, and the truth is
rather that their complexity as yet baffled the artist's
skill. In Italy, Carpaccio, Benozzo Gozzoli and Perugino,
and the German and Flemish painters Schongauer, Dürer
and Van der Weyden, charm us by the brilliance and

purity of their colour rather than by its subtlety or truth.
Yet a certain hardness, a want of blending is the more
noticeable to us, who can contrast it with the maturer
colouring of their successors.

Again, many of these early painters, as we have seen,
knew little of atmospheric or aerial perspective, by
means of which the effect of distance on colour is
expressed. They painted distant objects as brilliant as
those in the foreground, disregarding the fact that,
according as things recede from the eye, they become
not only smaller but changed in colour, generally faded
and dulled by the intervening veil of atmosphere, until
at last they are lost in a haze of blue. The distance in
such pictures is generally defined and airless. A simple
test of this blurring of colour by distance may be found
in watching a red cart or tram receding down a long
street. Its colour becomes little by little fainter and
dimmer, and at last it is impossible to see that it is
actually a bright red, though our knowledge that it is
so sharpens our eyes and perhaps helps to deceive them.
The temptation to the painter then is to paint a distant
red cart red, because of his knowledge that it would so
appear if close at hand. This effect of distance on
colour came only gradually to be understood. Landscape backgrounds were rendered indeed with rather
less of precision and minuteness than foreground or
middle distance, and with somewhat paler colouring,
but the actual changes of colour by distance were only
realised in the sixteenth century.

The question of aerial perspective is intimately connected with that of tone. In painting a picture it is not
enough for the artist to imitate faithfully the actual colour
of each object within his range of vision, the bright blue
of the sky, the intense green of the grass, the huntsman s

scarlet coat.   Each of these colours he might copy with the utmost fidelity, but his canvas would present a series of pictures, not a picture, for there would be no unity, no connection, truth perhaps of isolated tints, but no general truth of colour.   This, we have seen, was the mistake of all early painters.   Tone, a word continually on the lips of modern artists and critics, implies the relation of all the colours to each other as determined by the amount of light which each reflects, or, to use a scientific term, the " value " of the colour in the scheme of the whole.   The artist knows that a huntsman's coat is of a bright and glowing scarlet, but the knowledge will serve him nothing.   He must actually forget it, and consider the scarlet coat merely as a colour patch, whose intensity and brilliance, whose very hue is determined relatively to its surroundings.   It may appear as a dark patch against a brilliant sky, or as a brightly lighted spot or mass of warm colour in sombre surroundings.   Put a piece of red geranium against a gray wall with the light in front of it, and then hold it up against the bright sky.   In the first case it will appear a bright red ; in the second it will look almost black, all its colour faded when opposed to the brilliant light behind it.   It is the painter's business to observe these modifications of local colour, and in seeking truth of effect to attain it by accepting no colour as absolute, but to regard the scene before him as an area of lighted space, in which every colour is seen in its relation to the other colours and to the whole.   A colour that is out of tone, too brilliantly lighted or too strong in proportion to the rest of the picture, should affect the eye just as a false note in music hurts the ear.   Colour values are to the painter what harmonies are to the musician.   Strict truth of tone is the aim of the modern colourist, who looks back to Velasquez and the Dutchmen rather than to the more purely decorative colourists of the Renaissance.

Splendour of colouring is not produced merely by the use of brilliant local colours. There is all the difference in the world between colours and colour, between a number of bright, unblended tints promiscuously spotted together in a kind of patch-work, and a consistent colour-scheme. In nature objects do not appear as simple masses of hard and uniform colour, but are broken into subtle gradations of endless variety, every tint borrowing something from its neighbour, every surface displaying reflections and counter-reflections, every colour exerting its influence by relation or contrast. The gradual realisation of these facts prepared the way for the first great colourists, Titian, Veronese and Correggio in the South, Rubens and Rembrandt in the North. The change was no sudden one. We may trace in Venetian art the gradual development of colour in the work of Giovanni Bellini and his pupils Giorgione and Titian, greater breadth and freedom, increased boldness and more perfect harmony proclaiming the " New Manner."

What is it then that distinguished the Venetian as a colour-school above all others of that time? Chiefly this, that in addition to their warm and brilliant tints they further bathed everything in a flood of rich golden light. It was frankly a convention. It is but seldom that the world glows as in their pictures. Nor indeed did they always employ brighter colours or a larger choice of colours than other painters ; on the contrary, they made frequent use of black, which is rarely found in early art. Tintoretto's paradox that black and white are the most beautiful colours is comprehensible before such pictures as Titian's *Man with a Glove* in the

Louvre, or Moroni's *Lawyer* in the National Gallery. It is only the great colourists who understand that black and white do not imply absence of colour. The black of velvet, silk or brocade, as the Venetians painted it, is as vibrating and rich, as luminous and satisfying, as any crimson or purple. Equally many of them gained their finest effects by means of a few colours only, a simple palette. In Titian's *Crowning with Thorns* in the Munich Gallery he has used only four colours, black and white, red and orange ; yet the effect is rich and striking, and if the tints used in many a picture of splendid colour-effect be counted, they will often prove but a poor half-dozen. Typical examples of the opulence of Venetian colouring are Titian's *Presentation of the Virgin*, Bordone's *Fisherman presenting the Ring of St. Mark to the Doge* and Tintoretto's *Miracle of St. Mark*, all in the Academy at Venice. The brilliant crimsons, yellows and blues are harmonised in a flood of golden light. In colour Paul Veronese differs in some respects from his Venetian contemporaries, and obtains equal brilliance by other means. He delights in cool blues and grays where Titian used warm browns and reds, and the light in which he bathes his colours suggests the silvery effect of early morning rather than the glowing gold of sunset. We find these same silver harmonies in many of Tintoretto's pictures, notably in his wonderful *Bacchus and Ariadne* in the Ducal Palace, the cool shimmering light of which contrasts curiously with the golden glow of his *Miracle of St. Mark*. Moretto also uses these cool gray or silver tones.

Rubens, the inheritor of the Venetian tradition, stands almost alone in the North for the boldness and originality of his colouring. No one painted with greater fearlessness and self-confidence. He saw colour in everything,

TINTORETTO

BACCHUS AND ARIADNE

and used it with the greatest audacity and decorative effect, delighting in warm yellows, browns, crimsons and even scarlet, a colour rarely used by the Venetians. Passing from his sumptuous canvases to the quieter pictures of his Dutch contemporaries we again find a strong feeling for colour, but differently expressed. Rembrandt at the head of the School is as individual as Titian or Rubens. With him, as with Tintoretto and Correggio, colour and vigorous yet subtle chiaroscuro are inseparably bound up. In his pictures local colour is often lost in depths of luminous shadow. Broadly speaking, the chief characteristic of Dutch colouring is its fidelity and truth to nature. Not one of the Dutch painters but was a colourist, and this feeling for colour redeems many a coarse and unpleasant scene, and compensates for the frequent lack of beauty of face and form. The little genre scenes of Metzu, Terburg and De Hoogh are often gems of exquisite and harmonious colour, with something of the brilliance of enamel. Nothing can surpass the faultless colouring, deep, rich and glowing of Terburg's *Trumpeter handing a Dispatch* in the Hague, or De Hoogh's *Interior of a Dutch House* in the National Gallery. In their painting of satin, velvet or fur, it was not only the colour but the very texture of the material they succeeded in reproducing. Terburg's white satin is as marvellous as De Hoogh's black velvet.

When we compare the pictures of such colourists as Titian, Correggio, Rubens, Rembrandt, Watteau, Gainsborough, Turner, Delacroix, we find no two alike in their use of colour, though all are more or less true to nature. The great colourist never indeed aims merely at truth to nature, though his colour is always suggested by her. It has been said that colour may be either brilliant or

I

harmonious, but is always sufficiently like nature if it does not offend the spectator. Truth is not the last word in colour. It is not a matter of truth but of feeling. That colour can at times come perilously near the verge of extravagance and exaggeration may be seen in some of Turner's work. His most splendid effects are sometimes frankly impossible, atmospheric paradoxes, the dreams of his studio inspired by nature. He seizes upon sunset hues which in reality last but a fraction of a moment, and throws them in splendid profusion upon his canvas. Yet it would be hard to say that the whole effect is so unlike nature as to offend the eye, or that it is not justified by its beauty. It is the privilege of the artist to see farther than the rest of his fellows. Turner's reply to the lady who complained that she could not find in nature all the colours he had painted in his pictures, "Don't you wish you could, madam?" is based on a fuller understanding of the painter's province than was the criticism. Perhaps more is to be learned of the magic of colour in nature from Turner, especially in his water-colours, than from any other painter.

It is a common mistake to suppose that fine colour is necessarily gay, or that the best colour-effects are always the most striking. Turning from the pictures painted in the pure unbroken tints of the early Italian or Flemish masters to those of our own day, there is at first sight a loss of brilliance. In so far as this is due to the modern painter's greater feeling for truth of tone, the loss is more than compensated, but it sometimes happens that this modern practice of painting in broken tints leads in un-skilful hands to a certain smeariness, producing a dirty or muddy effect of colour. One of the aims of the English Pre-Raphaelite painters, disgusted with the brown, sad colouring of their contemporaries, was to ob-

INTERIOR

tain truth to nature by the use of purer colour. Returning to the methods of the primitive Florentine and Flemish masters, they faithfully matched the local colour of every object in their pictures, sacrificing, however, unity of effect and achieving in consequence only partial truth. Even among quite modern painters there are some who, like Leighton, have never freed themselves from this "tyranny of local colour." Again, the colour of a picture is often called brilliant when it is really tawdry, dull because it is quiet, exaggerated when it is merely bold. Pictures of the East, with their unfamiliar scale of colour and lighting, are apt to strike the untravelled spectator as crude and unnatural. In the same way, hot, violent tints are mistaken for rich, warm colour, while cool, pearly tones appear to some cold and lifeless. As fine effects have been gained by the use of the colder colours blue and gray as by the admittedly warmer reds, yellows and orange. It is well known that Gainsborough painted his famous *Blue Boy* in the Duke of Westminster's collection as a challenge to Reynolds, who had declared that a picture could not be made out of a cold colour while we get the effect of a hot summer day from many a modern landscape painted in a key of blues, grays and greens, without one touch of warm red or yellow.

In nothing, perhaps, does an artist show his personal genius for colour more than in his painting of flesh. There is every variety of complexion in art as in nature, from the healthy, ruddy flesh of Rubens to the green anaemic faces of Burne-Jones, from Giorgione's brown-faced *Shepherd* and his golden-limbed *Venus* to the pink and white waxen creations of Netscher and Van der Werff. In the painting of flesh the Venetians and Correggio are still unsurpassed. We find in them for the first time not only the colour, but the actual texture of warm living

flesh.   There is no finer flesh-painting in the world than
Correggio's *Antiope* in the Louvre.   In many pictures by
the Venetians and Rubens we find admirable contrasts
between the fair skin of the women and the brown sun-
burnt faces and limbs of the men.   In Titian's *Holy
Family* in the National Gallery the Madonna and Child
are admirably set off by the swarthy shepherd boy who
kneels before them.   This rich flesh-painting is in striking contrast with the hard, brick-red flesh of Giulio
Romano and the Carracci, the greenish grays of Bor-
gognone or the brown of Leighton's nudes.   Rubens's
magnificent rendering of flesh may be studied in all his
pictures.   Here too he followed the Venetians, adding
to their lustre and brilliancy something more of warm
red.   As Guido Reni said, he surely must have mixed
blood with his colours.   He made frequent use, too, of
crimson shadows, under eyes, nose, chin, and between
the fingers.   In this he was followed by Van Dyck and
the English painters Reynolds and Romney, who sometimes even defined the features with a red line.

CHAPTER XIII

LIGHT AND SHADE

LIGHT and Shade, or Chiaroscuro, is in nature almost inseparable from colour, and the painter can hardly see them apart. But from the point of view of the spectator of a picture, as opposed to that of the artist, chiaroscuro may fairly be considered separately.

Strongly defined light and shade is by no means necessary in pictorial art. Pure line drawing and purely decorative painting have little of it. The artists of Japan, whether working in black and white or in colours, achieve the most astoundingly successful rendering of solid form without the use of shadows. It is the tradition of Japanese art to rely solely upon outline and flat colour to express form. Greek vase-painting is also shadowless and flat. Early fresco-painting and some of the most successful mural painting of modern times consists in the use of broad flat masses treated decoratively with little modelling or relief. But European painting relies on the help of light and shade wherever modelling or the effect of projecting and receding masses is required. The use of light and shade is indeed the basis of all modelling and all relief. By its means the subtlest and most delicate gradations of form may be rendered, even to the different planes upon flat surfaces.

In its narrower but more generally accepted sense, the term chiaroscuro is used to express the broadest and strongest effects of light and shadow over the whole picture. After mentally eliminating line and colour, we can judge how far the effect is obtained by the distribution and the proportion of the light and shadow, always bearing in mind that it is only at some little distance from a picture that its scheme of chiaroscuro can be adequately appreciated.

Reynolds, when travelling in Italy as a student, was especially interested in the chiaroscuro of the great Venetian masters and jotted down in his notebook his own method of studying these effects detached from all other considerations. "When I observed," he writes, "an extraordinary effect of light and shade in any picture, I took a leaf out of my pocket-book and darkened every part of it in the same gradation of light and shade as the picture, leaving the white paper untouched to represent the light, and this without any attention to the subject, or to the drawing of the figures. By this means you may likewise remark the various forms and shapes of those lights, as well as the objects on which they are flung, whether a figure or the sky, or a white napkin, animals, or utensils, often introduced for this purpose only. . . . Such blotted paper held at a distance from the eye will strike the spectator as something excellent for the disposition of light and shadow, though it does not distinguish whether it is a history, a portrait, a landscape, dead game or anything else ; for the same principles extend to every branch of the art."

Whether we use the term chiaroscuro in its wider or its more limited sense, the question is always one of gradations of light. All colour is modified by the degree of light or shadow falling upon it, as we noticed in the case of the red geranium held first against the light and then against a gray background. The amount and proportion of light or shade in a picture will of course depend upon the choice of the painter. He may consciously disregard chiaroscuro almost entirely to give an impression of flatness. He may emphasise and exaggerate it beyond nature by the artificial devices of the studio, cutting off the light entirely on one side and concentrating it forcibly elsewhere. Any portrait will show the way in which it has been employed. If the light falls from the side the shadows cast by the features will be so disposed as to give the due sense of relief, but they will differ from the deep shadows under eyes, nose and chin cast by a top light such as Hoppner, Raeburn and Lawrence continually used to obtain an easy and forcible effect of relief and modelling. Or he may prefer full outdoor effects, with the sunlight distributed broadly over the whole or falling fitfully from behind heavy clouds, touching near or distant objects with its gleams.

We find examples of every method of chiaroscuro in a picture-gallery. Early pictures, especially those of the Florentine School, show the very simplest treatment of light and shade. This is partly due to the fact that the painters were accustomed to cover large wall-surfaces where, whether in mosaic or fresco, a broad flat treatment is the most effective. Just as a wall-paper with a pattern in high relief offends the eye, so wall-painting requires only so much relief as will make it intelligible. Giotto, skilled observer as he was, did not attempt to give the effect of light and shadow caused by the fire in his fresco of *St. Francis before the Soldan* in S. Croce at Florence. The blazing fire is represented as a dark mass against a lighter background, casting neither shadow nor reflection. In some early German pictures the flames of burning candles are mere touches of gold giving no suggestion of light. The Madonnas and Saints of the primitive Tuscan painters live in a shadowless world of their own. Where chiaroscuro is attempted it is generally quite arbitrary, the light falling from different sides with no pretence to consistency.

The Venetian and Flemish painters employed a more vigorous chiaroscuro from the beginning, and the oil method which was introduced in the fifteenth century lent itself to broader effects and greater depth of shadow. The "New Manner" of the sixteenth century, as Vasari justly termed it, consisted largely in a greater unity of light and shade, a stronger feeling for modelling and relief, by means of which a far closer semblance to nature was obtained. With many artists chiaroscuro came to be no longer merely an aid to the representation of form but a source of aesthetic effect, an end in itself. The great chiaroscurists, Leonardo, Correggio, Tintoretto and Rembrandt, deliberately sought and found beauty in new and daring effects of light and shade. Compare them with their predecessors and the contrast is striking. Instead of being uniformly distributed, the light is broken up so that but a fraction of the picture receives it, while the rest is in half shadow or deep, impenetrable gloom. According to Reynolds the practice of the later Venetians appeared to be to allow not above a quarter of the picture for the light, including both principal and secondary lights, another quarter to be kept as dark as possible and the remainder in half shadow. "Rubens," he remarks, "seems to have admitted rather more light than a quarter and Rembrandt much less, scarcely an eighth ; by this conduct Rembrandt's light is extremely brilliant, but it costs too much, and the rest of the picture is sacrificed to this one object."

The gradual appreciation of the aesthetic value of chiaroscuro opened out new and wider possibilities for pictorial art.   By its means, objects and scenes, however fair in themselves, are endowed with an added halo of romance and beauty.   Early art, in which everything was clear, hard and defined, knew nothing of the mystery-pro-ducing power of effects of half light and deep obscurity. High lights gained an added brightness from contrast with deepest gloom.   Shadows were found to be not black masses but luminous and full of colour.   The in-fluence of reflections, direct and indirect, on colour began to absorb attention.   Painting gained both in scope and complexity.   These were not the discoveries of one generation or of a single school, but little by little the search into the mysteries of light and shade by the pioneers of chiaroscuro could not fail of its effect upon the art of painting.   Leonardo, as Vasari narrates, not content with his darkest shadows, laboured constantly to discover the ground tone of others still darker, to the end that the light might thus be rendered yet more brilliant.   The mysterious, unearthly effect of his *Vir-gin of the Rocks* in the Louvre is the result of this strong contrast between the bright light that illumines the faces and the deep obscurity of the surroundings. Unfortunately his use of deep shadow was not without its baneful influence on contemporary painters like Fra Bartolommeo, who in their endeavour to emulate Leon-ardo's effects of relief blackened their shadows to the everlasting detriment of their pictures.   To Leonardo also is attributed the first deliberate adoption of indoor or studio light, with its carefully prearranged effects.

Tintoretto went further, and to gain greater effect often made use of artificial light.   His habit was to model little figures in wax or clay, placing them after-wards in a box with a lighted candle in order to study their chiaroscuro.   In his hands light and shade became powerful instruments of dramatic expression.   Many of his finest works at Venice, the *Bacchus and Ariadne* in the Ducal Palace, the *Annunciation* in the Scuola di S. Rocco and the *Marriage of Cana* in the Salute, owe their chief beauty to the vigorous and forceful chiaroscuro.   Indeed many of Tintoretto's pictures depend entirely for their effect on his peculiar treatment of light and shade, in which local colour is entirely drowned.   In the *Bacchus and Ariadne* the silvery light plays over the figures and gleams on the naked flesh with subtle and delicate transparency.   The complicated and effective lighting in the *Marriage of Cana* especially excited the interest of the youthful Reynolds.   " This picture," he writes in his notebook, " has the most natural light and shadow that can be imagined.   All the light comes from the several windows over the table.   The woman who stands and leans forward to have a glass of liquor is of great service ; she covers part of the tablecloth so that there is not too much white in the picture, and by means of her strong shadows she throws back the table and makes the perspective more agreeable.   But that her figure might not appear like a dark inlaid figure on a light ground her face is light, her hair masses with the ground, and the light of her handkerchief is whiter than the tablecloth." If Tintoretto uses light to produce dramatic effect, and Leonardo to enhance the subtle mystery of his creations, with Correggio it is the chief source of beauty, softening and sweetening all it touches.   He is the Italian Rembrandt in his feeling for chiaroscuro, but a Rembrandt converted from gloom to sunshine, joyous, youthful, serene.

The use of a forcible and striking chiaroscuro was carried beyond all legitimate limits by the followers and imitators of the great Italian chiaroscurists, who in their

THE MARRIA

[Salute, Venice

GE OF CANA

WOMAN TAKEN IN ADULTERY

endeavours to outvie their predecessors made for themselves a world of theatrically contrasted light and darkness, peopled by grandiose, superhuman giants. Caravaggio is the head of these painters of extravagant effects, who earned for themselves the name of the "Tenebrosi," or Painters of Darkness. The Spanish painter Ribera, too, who founded his art on Correggio and Caravaggio, painted powerful and interesting effects of light and shade, which give his pictures a peculiar interest. But in less capable hands the strong shadows used to enhance the effect of brilliant lighting ceased to be luminous, vibrating and full of colour, and became cold, black and heavy. Vigorous chiaroscuro degenerated into mere melodrama.

It is when we come to Rembrandt that the whole mysterious beauty of chiaroscuro, with its power to lend a charm and dignity to the meanest subject, is revealed. In the work of his mature years he uses a system of inclosed radiance, the light breaking as it were from masses of deep and luminous shadow to fall keenly on some particular object. This rich envelope of golden-brown, transparent shadow added a new glory to the masterly characterisation and sure modelling of his figures. No one before him had succeeded in so subduing the powers of day and night and bidding each perform its appointed part in pictorial effect. Does Rembrandt's brilliance of light really cost too much, as Reynolds suggests? How is it possible to accede to the proposition in the face of such masterly treatment as is displayed in the *Woman taken in Adultery* in the National Gallery, the *Pilgrims of Emmaus* in the Louvre, the *Raising of the Cross* in Munich, and the vast series of portraits of his middle and later periods, in which the light is focussed upon the most important passage in the picture? Rembrandt's peculiar and personal treatment of chiaroscuro naturally excited a host of followers and imitators. It is largely owing to his influence that the Dutch School is renowned for striking and poetical treatment of light. De Hoogh and Vermeer of Delft are almost modern in their treatment of light and shade. De Hoogh furnishes his simple, almost bare interiors with golden sunlight and rich colour. Vermeer delights in cool tones, blues and grays, and the effect of light pouring in through latticed window on wall and furniture. The same mysterious magic redeems the somewhat vulgar scenes of Adrian van Ostade and Brouwer, lifting them into the realm of beauty.

Artists were not slow to perceive that by means of light and shade every subject could be rendered interesting and beautiful. Reynolds's reply, when at the height of his fame he was asked how he could bear to paint the ugly cocked-hats, bonnets and wigs of his own time, "They all have light and shadow," must have seemed obvious enough to the great artist who, as a youth, had darkened the leaves of his pocket-book as he sat at the feet of Tintoretto and Veronese in Venice. Even more have the painters of still life, of household pots and pans, the implements and contents of the larder, proved that nothing is really common or unclean where observation and sympathy combine to perpetuate it in the form of art.

Allusion has been made already to the veil or *envelope* of atmosphere intervening between the object and the eye. The nature or quality of this *envelope* depends on the amount of light upon it. This in its turn is determined by such considerations as the natural purity of the air, the time of day, the season of the year. According as the light is pure and white or tinged with

TERBURG

[National Gallery

THE PEACE OF MÜNSTER

Hanfstängl photo

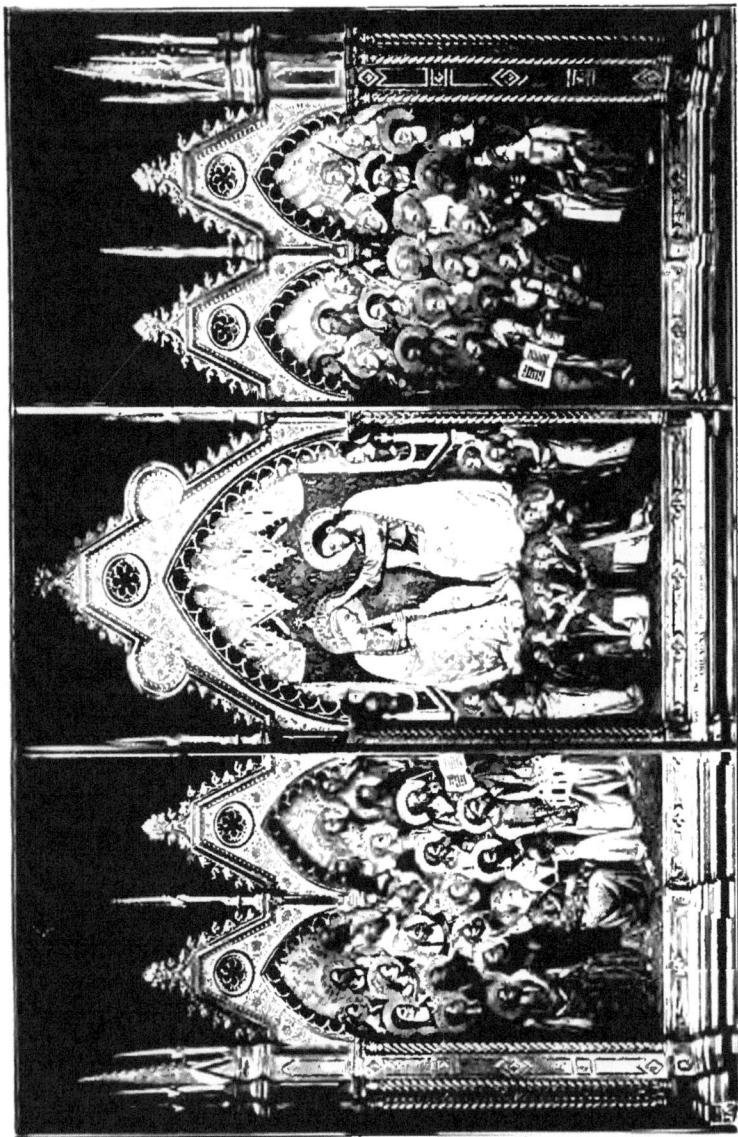

ASCRIBED TO ORCAGNA

CORONATION OF THE VIRGIN

[National Gallery]

Hanfstängl photo]

colour, the general effect will be cool or glowing.   The
light of early morning is perceptibly colder and more
silvery than the golden illumination of late afternoon.
Again, the lighting of a picture may be natural or
artificial, the light of the studio or of the open air, and
its influence upon near or distant objects must be correctly rendered.   Truth of tone, or correct colour-value,
for it is the same problem in another form, depends on
the careful analysis and due appreciation of light, for
tone is a question of the quantity of light reflected by
any given colour, which proves how intimate is the connection between colour and chiaroscuro.

Light is the great unifying element in a picture.   By
consistent rendering of light and shade all the parts of
the picture are brought into perfect relationship.   Compare such a picture as the *Coronation of the Virgin* in
the National Gallery, ascribed to Orcagna, with its tier
upon tier of saints and martyrs rising one behind the
other, with Terburg's *Peace of Münster* in the same collection.   In the work of the Florentine there are no
subtle gradations of tone, the light is inconsistent, being
uniformly distributed over the foremost and most distant
figures. Those in the background are as brightly lighted
as those in the foreground.   In a word, there is no
general scheme of light, each figure has been considered
by itself.   In Terburg's *Peace of Münster*, on the contrary, there is a well-considered scheme of light, a definite light-centre, to which every tone in the picture is
related.   He distinguishes with marvellous delicacy of
tone the subtle differences between the figures in front
and those behind and at the sides, giving to each its due
proportion of light.   The picture is a whole, not an
aggregation of parts.

It is this recognition of the unity of chiaroscuro which

characterises modern art, and is the special heritage bequeathed by Velasquez to his artistic successors of to-day. Only by regarding the scene before him as a whole can a painter attain unity of *ensemble*. With Velasquez this unity was a paramount consideration. He never looked at one part of the subject he was painting without keeping in mind the general impression of the whole, the impression made upon the eye by a first glance. In this he differed from the older masters, the Venetians and Rubens, who sought unity only by means of line and decoratively disposed masses of colour, and practically ignored consistency of lighting and the finer subtleties of tone. Titian even went so far as to paint figures in full sunlight against a sunset sky. But there is painter's as well as poet's licence, and even in Watteau's most beautiful park and garden scenes the lighting is never that of the open air.

It was in revolt against the general use of the subdued artificial light of the studio and in favour of more natural light effects, that a school of painters arose in France some thirty years ago, and has since found sympathisers in every land. The Plein-airists, as they are called, insisted on painting nature in the open air, and would hear nothing of studio landscapes. Intensely sensitive to momentary changes of light, which obviously require great rapidity of execution, they succeeded in arresting and perpetuating effects unknown within doors, where the light remains long unchanged and is comparatively unaffected by considerations of hour or weather. The movement was directed in the first instance against the practice of painting landscapes almost entirely within doors, and consequently under conditions of light and atmosphere which could not possibly exist in nature. Even in winter the glass studios of the Plein-airists admit as nearly as possible the full light of the open air. Above all, they set themselves to interpret directly the effect of strong sunshine upon natural objects, its power of swallowing all local colour in a uniform silver haze. It was a step still further in advance when the principles of *plein air* were applied to indoor subjects. This new conception of light accounts no doubt, to some extent at least, for the absence in a collection of modern pictures of the low tones characteristic of the old masters. The general impression is distinctly brighter, even when we allow for the darkening influence of time. This more rational lighting of modern painting is indeed a revolution from the stereotyped "gallery tones" of the eighteenth century, but it needed all the artistic courage of a Constable or a Manet to break down a tradition so depressing and absurd.

CHAPTER XIV

COMPOSITION

IT often happens when standing before a picture which appears to be well drawn and pleasantly coloured, that we are conscious of something wanting. There seems to be no true centre, no rest for the eye, which loses itself in a maze of detail but gains no sense of unity or coherence. This is probably because the picture is not well put together, the various elements not combined so as to produce one perfect whole ; in a word, the composition is faulty. For the painter, like the musician, has certain materials which, by skilful arrangement, he converts into a work of art. The musician deals with sounds, the painter with form and colour. And in both cases the work of art, be it symphony or picture, is the result of the harmonious combination of these elements. It is not enough that it should contain passages of un-doubted beauty, if these be scattered and disconnected. A painter needs more than good draughtsmanship and a fine feeling for colour. He must also possess that sense of decorative proportion, of balance and unity, which prompts him to treat his picture as so much pattern, to weave his forms and colours into a well-considered scheme, in which all the parts are related to each other and to the whole. Many pictures lack this consistent disposition of their component parts, with the result that we have, as it were, on one canvas several pictures, but no picture.

The painter has thought more of each part, the *morceau*, than of the whole effect.

Unity of composition is attained by several means, of which, as we have seen, harmonious line and consistent chiaroscuro are the most important. The lines of a composition may repeat each other or be in direct contrast, but in either case they must be intimately related and lead up to the centre of the picture. Some pictures are knit together entirely by means of interlacing, harmonising lines, and though the scheme of light may be elementary and the colour spotted on almost as an afterthought, unity of composition may still be preserved. The composition of most modern pictures is chiefly an affair of the careful distribution of light, the painter seeking consistency of chiaroscuro and truth of tone before all else.

Unity of action is also an important factor in good composition. There should be only one centre of interest, one principal figure or group, to which the rest of the picture is subordinate. This unity of action was entirely disregarded by many of the early painters, who in their desire to tell a story graphically often introduced several scenes into the same picture. This is done with curious effect in the fresco of *The Church Militant* in the Spanish Chapel of S. Maria Novella in Florence, where the different incidents are not only piled on the top of each other, but the figures even vary in size to suit the exigencies of space. In Masaccio's fresco of *The Tribute Money* in the Brancacci Chapel three distinct incidents are narrated, though in this case without losing unity of pictorial effect, the middle group of Christ and his Apostles forming a true centre for the picture. Even Raphael in his *Transfiguration* makes two distinct centres, the scene of the actual Transfiguration on the

K

mountain and below, and, curiously enough in greater prominence, the secondary incident of the healing of the demoniac.   On the ceiling of the Sistine Chapel, Michelangelo represented the Temptation, Fall and Expulsion from the Garden of Eden in one compartment.   Though in such composite pictures unity of action is sacrificed, harmony of line and careful distribution of the masses help to preserve unity of composition.   In Michelangelo's fresco the graceful lines of the figures draw the whole together, and there is no sense of isolation or restlessness. In the centre is the tree, from one side of which the tempter stretches out an arm to Eve, while Adam reaches for the fruit.   On the right the avenging angel drives the guilty pair from Eden.   The two groups, both composed of the same figures, balance one another perfectly, and the outstretched arms of the angel, the tempter and Adam link together the three principal masses.

A somewhat similar difficulty confronts the painter of a portrait-group, where no sitter will consent to take a subordinate position.   As we have seen, this problem had to be faced by the Dutch painters, when called upon to portray the members of some corporation or guild. To paint half a score of figures in a group may not be difficult, but where each insists on individual consideration and equal prominence pictorial unity becomes well-nigh impossible.   Many of these Regent pictures are nothing but charts, maps of faces, as it were.   But the best artists, Hals and Ravesteyn, overcame the difficulty, and by skilful grouping and clever lighting contrived to infringe neither their patrons' wishes nor their own sense of harmonious composition.

This difficulty of grouping several figures together was evaded by some of the early Italians, notably the Vivarini

MICHELANGELO

[SistineChapel, Rome]

THE TEMPTATION, FALL AND EXPULSION

Alinari photo]

RAPHAEL

THE CAMERA DELLA SEGNATURA

SHOWING THE PARNASSUS AND PART OF THE SCHOOL OF ATHENS

and Crivelli, who painted each figure of an altar-piece on a separate panel, uniting them afterwards in one common frame. In these " Anconas," where each figure appears in a separate framework, unity of composition is not attempted. Each saint is an independent being, bearing but the most superficial relation to any other. Gradually, however, the framework between the figures was done away with, and definite attempts at harmonious grouping were made.

It is obviously easier to compose a picture of few and simple materials, of but one or two figures, than to give coherence to a crowded scene. Yet even a picture of a single figure, a portrait, may be well or ill composed. It may crowd the frame, giving an uncomfortable sense of cramped space, or by being placed too much on one side or too high the figure may lose balance, and the picture seem lop-sided or top-heavy. How admirably some portraits seem to fit their frames, without a feeling of either emptiness or crowding. Velasquez has wonderfully contrived to make us feel the depth of space surrounding the figure in his portraits. It sometimes happens that a painter, having begun his picture, feels that his subject is confined by the size of the canvas, and to meet this adds strips on either side to give a greater sense of space. The fresco-painter has no such opportunity. The size and shape of his wall-space are unelastic, and his picture must be composed to fit them. Raphael's *Parnassus* and *Mass of Bolsena* in the Vatican are so finely composed that we scarcely realise how awkward were the spaces the painter was called upon to fill, a door cutting through the middle, leaving two difficult corners. Again, his designs in the spandrels of the ceiling of the Farnesina may well be studied as triumphs of spacing. But apart from the peculiar difficulties affecting the fresco-painter, the actual composing of even a single figure needs experience and knowledge of space-effect. We should have a sense of limitation and discomfort if, when designing a stooping figure, the artist so composed it that it would be impossible for it to stand upright, or in the case of a figure in suspended action there were no room for the completion of the movement.

Still greater is the difficulty before the artist who has to give unity to a complex, crowded scene, to bring order out of disorder, and this without giving the impression of too elaborate arrangement or painfully acquired effect. For this kind of composition Rubens had a perfect instinct. At first sight his *Lion Hunt* in Munich gives an impression of wild disorder, horses, men and lions in a tangle of limbs and weapons. This is, of course, the artist's intention, a consciously sought effect of chaos, in which in reality there is perfect order and harmony. His *Battle of the Amazons* in the same gallery, and his *Kermesse* in the Louvre, are extravagantly crowded scenes with figures in every variety of attitude admirably composed, though with little apparent effort. In all the maze of figures the effect is never confused. In such large elaborate compositions the artist has always to bear in mind the fact that a picture must make an effective impression at the first glance. There must be some centre on which attention is instinctively focussed. Afterwards the spectator may unravel the intricacies of the composition, and enjoy the inter-relation of all the parts. It is here that Tintoretto's great *Paradise* in the Ducal Palace fails. There is too much for the eye to take in at a glance, and no point of vantage on which it can rest in the welter of figures. The general impression is one of scattered confusion.

As illustrating the different means by which painters

[Munich]

RUBENS

THE LION HUNT

[Hanfstängl photo]

JAN STEEN

FAMILY OF THE PAINTER

achieve unity of compositon, we may compare the apparently careless, natural grouping of such pictures as Jan Steen's *Family of the Painter* at the Hague, *The Haymakers* of Bastien - Lepage or Millais's *Carpenter's Shop* with the formal symmetrical arrangement of Memlinc's *St. John Altar-piece*, Raphael's *Sposalizio* or Titian's *Assumption*. In the first instances the composition appears easy and unpremeditated. There is no attempt at symmetry, and the impression made by the pictures is one of spontaneity and truth to life. We can well believe that Jan Steen painted his picture from what he saw in the parlour of his own inn, where he and his friends were making merry. *The Haymakers* is a lifelike representation of a man and woman resting from their labours under the glare of the noonday sun. The scene in the *Carpenter's Shop*, where the whole interest centres round the child Christ, who has hurt his hand on a nail, is one that the painter might have observed for himself in some modern workshop. How differently it would have been treated by one of the old masters! But for all the apparent ease of grouping in such pictures, a little research will in every case reveal the painter's care for order and balance. In well-composed pictures every detail is arranged with a view to the whole, every figure, every attitude duly considered, and often the most apparently natural composition is the result of infinite study and reflection. By way of testing the composition, take away or transpose a single figure and the effect will often be irretrievably marred ; add another, and the result may be to spoil the whole balance of the picture.

When we turn to the second group of pictures our impressions are quite different. Instead of natual grouping we find formal, orderly arrangement, and often perfect symmetry. In the *Sposalizio* the group of the

Virgin and her maidens on the left is repeated on the right by that of Joseph and the disappointed suitors. In the middle stands the high priest, who joins the hands of bride and bridegroom, and the temple behind, with the steps leading up to it, completes the well-balanced composition. The reason for this formal arrangement is not far to seek. Such pictures as these were painted to hang in a definite place, to form part of the decoration of some church, where, from over high altar or side-chapel, they could be advantageously seen by the wor-shippers. Under these circumstances it is evident that the painter is not free to compose his picture independ-ently of all considerations beyond his personal taste. A picture painted for a definite position must be designed to harmonise with its surroundings ; in a word, architec-tonic conditions must be fulfilled. The main lines of the composition must repeat and carry on the lines of the building, or consciously contrast with them to give variety. It is essential that something of the symmetrical proportions of the architecture should find an echo in the picture painted to adorn it, that the painter should bring the grouping of the figures within his frame to some extent into harmony with the lines and masses without. When Titian composed his great *Assumption* for the high altar of a church in Venice, he little dreamed that one day the picture would be removed from its setting and hung in a picture-gallery, where its intention and decorative fitness are lost and forgotten. He instinctively adopted a less formal arrangement for an easel picture intended to hang upon the wall of a private palace, as was the *Bacchus and Ariadne* now in the National Gal-lery, where the composition is irregular and unbalanced almost to confusion.

The fresco-painter in particular is bound by considera-

MILLAIS

THE CARPENTER'S SHOP

Private Possession

　　　　　　　　　　　　　　　　　　　　　　　　　[Academy, Venice

ASSUMPTION OF THE VIRGIN

tions of the building he is called upon to adorn.   He
too must design his pictures so as to obtain the best
effect from the place where they will be most frequently
seen.   For this purpose the simplest composition is often
the best, and a careful arrangement of lines tells better
than elaborate effects of colour or chiaroscuro.   Leonardo's *Last Supper* is not only a magnificent composition
in itself, but is admirably designed for the end-wall of a
spacious refectory, where as they sat at meals the monks
could see the long table of the picture forming, as it
seemed, part of the room itself, and, like the high table
in a college hall, slightly raised above the rest.   It was
obviously convenient for this purpose to range the
Apostles on the far side of the table, facing the room,
with Christ in the middle ; and to vary this long line the
painter has broken it into four groups, uniting them,
however, with consummate skill through the expressive
action of the hands.   Veronese's *Marriage of Cana* in
the Louvre, and his *Feast in the House of Levi* in the
Venice Academy, though not frescoes, were painted for
a similar position, and much of their purpose is missed
where they now hang among other pictures in a gallery.
Correggio's desire to annihilate the architectural limits of
the dome in the Cathedral of Parma, to pierce it, as it
were, and make the spectator believe he was gazing up
into space, was a bold device on the part of the painter,
a *tour de force* of perspective and composition, which in
any other hands could scarcely have hoped to succeed.
The antithesis of this kind of illusory composition is
one often found in Venetian churches, where the painter
by a trick of perspective makes a flat ceiling appear
elaborately vaulted.

    With regard, however, to the formal grouping of the
old Italian pictures, it is only fair to remember that in

many cases the artists were following old-established
traditions of composition favoured by the Church, from
which they but gradually escaped to a more individual
conception.   Not until after studying some of the early
sculptured reliefs and mosaics is it possible to realise
how closely the painters of the Renaissance adhered to
the designs of their predecessors.   The traditional composition of the *Baptism of Christ*, as it may be seen in
mosaic in the Baptistery of St. Mark at Venice, was
repeated with little change until the sixteenth century.
Christ stands in the river in the middle of the picture, on
one side St. John the Baptist from a rocky bank pours
water over his head, on the other kneel three little angels
holding Christ's garments.   So Giotto rendered this
incident in the Arena Chapel at Padua, and even Bellini
kept to the old arrangement in his altar-piece at Vicenza,
adding, however, a beautiful mountainous landscape setting and a luminous sky.   Again, the customary composition of the scene of the Transfiguration varied little
from the sixth century to the sixteenth.   Duccio's little
Transfiguration in the National Gallery is scarcely less
Byzantine than its prototypes, and even Raphael two
hundred years later repeated the same grouping with but
slight alteration.   New subject-matter alone called forth
the artist's powers of invention and arrangement.   When
Giotto painted the legend of St. Francis in twenty-eight
scenes on the walls of the Upper Church at Assisi, he
had no older models to turn to.   No painter before him
had translated the well-known story into pictorial form,
and created a traditional rendering to be copied with
little variation for centuries to come.   Giotto was obliged
to compose for himself, and with wonderful skill he
designed these dramatic though simple scenes, grouping
his figures in the most expressive attitudes and uniting

them in some common interest. Again, when mythological and historical subjects came into fashion, there
existed no established forms to follow, and artists were
forced to originate their designs.

In many pictures it will be found that the composition
can be inclosed within some simple and geometrical
figure, such as a triangle or pyramid. Sometimes, indeed,
it seems based upon the use of two such figures of
different dimensions. Fra Bartolommeo was the first who
deliberately adopted the pyramidal form of composition
to gain grand monumental effect. Nearly all his altar-
pieces are designed on this principle. Raphael borrowed
it from him, as we see in *La Belle Jardinière* and many of
the pictures of his second period. Titian uses it with
supreme effect in his *Entombment* in the Louvre, and
Giorgione, though in a somewhat irregular form, in his
Fête Champêtre in the same gallery. By the seventeenth
century pyramidal composition had become almost a
canon of art in Italy, and was repeated to weariness by
Raphael's imitators. The pyramid, indeed, like any other
regular figure, gives a sense of rest to the eye, and carries
with it a suggestion of strength and dignity. Even in
the less formal compositions of the Dutch masters and
of modern painters the grouping is often arranged somewhat on the lines of an irregular pyramid. Hogarth indeed in his " Analysis of Beauty " recommended it as
the best form of composition.

CHAPTER XV

TREATMENT

IT must be obvious, even to the most casual observer, that painters appear to see the world of form and colour from which they derive their material in many different ways, from infinitely varying points of view, and record their observations in every conceivable manner. One seems to regard his canvas as a mirror in which he strives to reflect with unswerving fidelity and care the things around him, whatever they may be. Another, apparently treating nature as a storehouse, selects such familiar objects and scenes as appeal to him and invests them with a beauty and distinction all his own. Yet another gives us fanciful unfamiliar effects suggestive of dream-life rather than of the everyday world around us. And the question inevitably arises whether all these ways of looking at nature and of painting her are proper to the painter's art. What does he seek to attain ? What means may he employ ? With the limitations imposed by his medium how far can he hope to succeed ? And with the answers to these questions a number of much-abused terms are bound up—Realism, Idealism, Classicism, Naturalism, Impressionism—which are convenient enough to express certain broad tendencies or points of view, but fail at once if used as labels in a rigid system of picture classification.

One of the first questions to occur to most people in

looking at a picture is whether or not it resembles nature. Should not every picture resemble, even imitate nature, and if so, how closely can it do so? This is rudimentary criticism, but none the less of real importance.

In a sense all painting must from the necessity of the case imitate nature, but equally of necessity it can only do so to a limited extent. Painting is after all a deception, a trick, a convention by which objects in three dimensions are represented in terms of two only, by means of line, colour, and light and shade. The painter imitates nature in the sense that he takes natural forms for his models. But there, strictly speaking, imitation ends. Indeed, were it to be desired, complete imitation of nature is not to be attained in paint, if alone for the fact that the vast discrepancy in actual brilliance between the brightest pigments and the hues of nature can never be overcome. Even if colour photography were perfected its imitation of nature would be but partial. And further, the fact that the artist is a human being, not a machine, an individual with strong tastes and sympathies, implies that personal interpretation of nature which is the very essence of pictorial art. It is strange that the misconception of art as a slavish imitation of nature should have taken so strong a hold of men's minds. It is a fallacy hard to dispel. Burger expressed the whole truth when he wrote: " In the works which interest us the authors substitute themselves, so to speak, for nature. However commonplace the natural material may be, their perception of it is special and rare."

When discussing portraiture and landscape we noticed that no two artists see the same thing alike and consequently never render it in exactly the same way. Even such a consideration as that of short or long sight has its influence in this assertion of individuality. It may be

that, giving full rein to his fancy, the painter seeks rather
to emphasise and develop those qualities and characteristics in his subject which most appeal to his own sympathies.   These may tend strongly in one direction, in
that of an intensely emotional and personal interpretation rather than in faithful and detailed reproduction of
what his eyes record.   His training, the influences about
him may predispose him to such imaginative treatment.
His mind may be stored with images nobler, more inspired than those of his fellow-men.   He may see with
the eyes of the poet and invest all that he paints with the
glory of his vision.   His quest may be the unattainable
in art, and his triumph to approach it ever so distantly.
Such is the attitude of the Idealist.   On the other hand,
the painter may consciously strive to reproduce the
objects and scenes before him exactly as they appear to
his eye, omitting nothing, altering nothing, concealing
nothing in his quest after truth.   This point of view is
that of the Realist.

Every artist is inevitably something of an Idealist as
well as something of a Realist.   The terms cannot be
mutually exclusive.   We often hear it said that a subject
has been treated realistically or in a spirit of idealism,
and it is a common practice to divide all painters into
two great classes, Idealists and Realists.   This division
once accomplished to the satisfaction of the would-be
critic, his next step will almost inevitably be to consider
either the one or the other as the only true exponents of
art.   Yet each merely represents a different point of
view from which art may be regarded.   Even in so far
as these terms represent opposite tendencies, misunder-
standing has arisen through the confounding of quite
alien issues.   In the minds of many Idealism is associated
with religious art, and applies to the spirituality of a

Perugino or an Ary Scheffer, quite overlooking the intensely realistic treatment of religious subjects by a Roger van der Weyden or a Holman Hunt. Others connect it with moral teaching, oblivious of the fact that Hogarth was both the greatest moralist and the sternest realist of his time. Others again confuse it with the sentimentality of a Carlo Dolci or a Greuze, or with the artificiality of a Le Brun or an Overbeck. In the same way Realism has become popularly identified with sensualism and vulgarity, with ugliness and deformity, heedless of the fact that it is connected with an attitude of mind, a point of view, and not with choice of subject.

However misleading such associations, there is certainly a great deal in the history of painting to account for their prevalence. Raphael expressed the true spirit of Idealism when he declared that he drew men and women, not as they were, but as they ought to be. This became the aim of the artists who succeeded him, but their forms were too often empty and exaggerated, devoid alike of natural truth and of ideal beauty. It came to be generally accepted as a principle that nature was always imperfect, weak or over-minute, and must be corrected by art. Reynolds, who was deeply imbued with Italian Idealism, declared that " the great artist will leave it to lesser men to paint the minute discriminations which distinguish one object of the same species from another, while he, like the philosopher, will consider nature in the abstract." Working in this spirit, many painters had no desire for searching truth to nature, but deliberately generalised everything they painted in the full belief that so they would achieve great art. These principles were often reduced to an absurdity by the would-be heroic painters of the eighteenth century in England and France. We find David, in his great picture of Ugolino and his two sons perishing of starvation in prison, investing the dying figures with the most perfect classical forms and proportions, well furnished with flesh and muscle, and carefully posed according to the ideas of composition accepted in his day.   This bastard idealism, though the very negation of truth to nature, was yet widely removed from the true idealism of the great imaginative painters of all times.

Idealism then in painting, taking the word in its broader sense, implies the free poetical interpretation of nature even at the sacrifice of literal truth.   And indeed the demonstration of naked truth is never the sole aim and end of art.   The idealist goes beyond it, sees farther, penetrates deeper into the soul of nature, his vision is more beautiful, more complete than ours.   There is indeed admittedly a point at which want of truth to nature becomes a fault, and the most daring painters have at times exceeded even the painter's licence.   But short of shocking the spectator who possesses some power of imagination, by the presentment of something entirely unfamiliar even to his mind, this want of truth will not in itself detract from the beauty of a picture.   It has been remarked with justice that but seldom in the history of painting has the exaggeration of untruthfulness, whether in form or colour, lost all that it had sought to win by splendour of effect and boldness of treatment.   One exception must indeed be made in pleading this only secondary importance of truth to nature.   When Turner imagined a castle for his *Rivers of France* and called it the Château of Amboise, it mattered little that it was so different from the real castle of that name as to be practically unrecognisable.   But with a portrait it is different. It is not that the mere copying of nature is sufficient here any more than in a landscape, but it is essential that the portrait should resemble the original. Even such irreconcilable Classicists as David and Ingres, devoted as they were to the pursuit of what was to be more beautiful, more sublime than nature, fully recognised the need for a more natural style, a greater realism in their portraits.

In direct contrast with the aim of the idealist is that of the painter who desires to reproduce faithfully what he sees, and values truth of effect more than imaginative qualities. The extreme of realism is reached when the effect achieved is that of a *trompe l'œil*, an illusion, cleverly contrived to cheat us into believing that art is nature, a painted surface a solid form. This trick, which from the days of Zeuxis has found its admirers, is successful only in proportion as it is inartistic. For, as we have seen, imitation of nature is not the intention of art. Even so great an artist as Veronese painted a number of these *trompe l'œil* in a villa near Castelfranco, which he was decorating for a Venetian nobleman. As you enter the hall, a page in the costume of the sixteenth century, slashed doublet and trunk hose, looks inquiringly at you from behind a half-open door. It is a moment before you realise that door and page exist only in paint. From a gallery running round one of the rooms, two ladies and a dog look down on the visitor. Again, ladies and gallery are but the result of skilfully manipulated paint on the flat wall. These illusions, designed by the great Venetian painter in a spirit of play, can obviously not be taken seriously. The sternest realist understands the limits of his art, and knows that truth to nature is merely a comparative term.

Truth in art has almost as many aspects as in morals or philosophy. The painter may understand it as truth of general effect, possibly to the neglect of truth of detail. A forest glade, a wide landscape, an interior with figures may be painted as they look when regarded as a whole in a momentary glance, before the eye has time to take in details. On this side of truth to nature Impressionism lies. The Realist of broad effects and the modern Impressionist aim at truth of aspect or impression before all else. Their object is to represent their impression of a scene received at a given moment, to record what they actually see rather than what by reasoning and closer examination they know. They paint appearances, not facts. The ordinary man looks at nature in the light of certain preconceived ideas, founded upon conventional standards of some kind, any departure from which is heresy. " To such the grass is always green, the sky blue, and those distant details which his memory helps to define, he honestly thinks he is actually seeing with his naked eye." The realist of impression rejects all such foregone conclusions, and is not afraid to paint grass purple if, owing to the peculiar effect of light or shadow, it so appears to him, though he knows it to be in fact green. Nor does he deliberately select the finest scenery or models and paint them only when they are beautifully illuminated or composed. To him truth is beauty in a very wide sense. And so he often chooses what are to the spectator at first sight un-familiar and unlovely phases of nature, seized at random and painted as they actually appear, not as the chromo-lithographist or photographer might arrange them. It is this seizing and rendering of the more fleeting and unfamiliar aspects of nature that shocks many people who see for the first time the pictures of Whistler, Manet, Claude Monet and the many painters who work in their traditions. But the very fact that a picture strikes the inexperienced eye as impossible and untrue is often merely evidence that it represents some aspect or mood of nature which the spectator has never had the power of seeing for himself. It often happens that a momentary effect of sunlight on cloud or hill appears strange and unnatural even in nature. It will be still more so when transferred to a picture, and it is not to be wondered at that one who has not seen it in nature will scarcely credit it in art.

In the same way as there is a realism of general effect, so is there also a realism of detail. The painter who treats his subject minutely and with elaborate detail is equally with the other seeking truth, but it is truth of fact and not truth of appearance. A modern critic has expressed it as the attempt to reproduce the appearance of things "seen as it were through a microscope, and afterwards painted at the proper distance more by memory of details previously discovered than by actual sight." The minute painting of detail in many Flemish and Italian pictures illustrates this attitude. When we look into a room we do not see everything at once. If the eyes be opened for a second only and then closed again, they receive but an impression more or less definite of the general effect. But if we look carefully round on every side, into every corner, making notes of the shape and colour and lighting of every single object within our range of vision, and then paint them as accurately as we can, the result will certainly be realistic. But such minute realism of detail is too often obtained at the sacrifice of the broader aspect of truth, truth of general effect.

For instance, the English Pre-Raphaelites, Holman Hunt and Millais, in the fervour of reaction against the vague generalisation of contemporary art, and following in the footsteps of their Italian predecessors of the

fifteenth century, deliberately emphasised and even exaggerated accuracy of detail and truth of local colour.
When Millais paints a heap of straw on the ground in
the corner of his *Return of the Dove* he does not give
the actual effect it would produce on the eye in that
position, but paints it as if the whole attention were
concentrated upon each wisp at a time.   It is the same
with his colouring.   Every patch of local colour is
painted as it looks independently of the whole effect.
In such pictures the eye can never lose and find itself
again, and pictorial unity is sacrificed to the excessive
elaboration of each part.   This tendency is carried to
excess in Holman Hunt's *Shadow of Death* at Man-
chester, where even the shavings on the floor are rendered
with a realism as minute and searching as it is weari-
some to the eye.

Such conscientious and unswerving fidelity demands
a treatment equally minute and painstaking.   Minute
treatment may indeed be combined with breadth of
effect, as in the best Dutch masters, Terburg and
Metzu.   Their delicacy and perfection of finish can
hardly be surpassed, yet the detail does not force itself
into notice.   Meissonier's finish is almost of the same
quality.   The brush strokes are so minute as to be
scarcely perceptible.   Yet there is nothing niggling.
The best of this scrupulously fine painting pleases as
much by its beautiful texture and richness of colour as
by its delicacy and sureness of technique.   But this is
not always the case.   Gerard Dou, for example, often loses
more than he gains by his extreme minuteness.   Carried to
excess the result seems laboured and affected, as if the
painter cared more for skill of hand than for artistic
presentment.   He is said to have spent days painting
only the handle of a broomstick.   Peter van Slingelandt's

CARMENCITA

work claimed to stand the test of a magnifying glass. He boasted that one of his small pictures occupied him three years, one month being devoted exclusively to the ruffles and frills of a single figure. The result is marvellous, but it is not art.

In the strongest contrast is the bold execution of those painters who have sought above all to give breadth of effect by dashing and vigorous brushwork. Hals, Rembrandt, especially in his maturity, Velasquez and Sargent display a sureness of eye and hand as remarkable as anything in the Microscopic School. The sense of power over the medium is even more apparent. The brush-marks are there for all to see just as the painter dashed them on with swift, nervous certainty. How audacious the handling in Sargent's *Carmencita*! There is strength and virility in such treatment that no other can suggest, and as fine a sense of completeness, of consummate achievement as is known in art. Hals's *Laughing Cavalier* is a magnificent example of vigorous brushwork combined with wonderful delicacy in the working out of the pattern of the dress. To gain the whole effect of such pictures, the spectator must stand at some little distance, when the patches and splashes of colour fall each into its due place in the general scheme. As Rembrandt remarked to some one who was looking too closely into one of his paintings, pictures are intended to be looked at, not smelled.

CHAPTER XVI

METHODS AND MATERIALS

MANY people who constantly visit galleries and even possess collections of their own, take little or no interest in the technical processes by which a picture is built up. Some indeed regard this side of painting as " scarcely superior to cookery." And indeed from the point of view of aesthetic enjoyment, there is no need to know exactly how a work of art has been produced. To others again, and especially to the painter, a considerable portion of his pleasure comes from this very consideration. As he alone fully understands, so he is perhaps alone able fully to appreciate the difficulties with which the artist has had to contend and his success in overcoming them. He will know exactly how each effect has been gained. Sometimes this technical side of painting may occupy the painter-critic too much, almost, it would seem, to the exclusion of aesthetic pleasure, but certainly as a rule it is too little understood by the layman.

The effect of a picture is largely determined by the materials used in painting it. As far as modern painting is concerned, most people can readily distinguish between oil, water-colour and pastel. But this elementary experience is of little use in a study of old pictures, painted before the discovery of these now well-known methods. In painting a picture the artist has to decide not only what pigments he will employ, but also the ground on which they are to be painted, and the medium by which he will apply them. These grounds or foundations are either of wood, canvas, plaster or copper; the mediums employed various animal and vegetable oils and resins, and water.

Several references have been made to fresco-painting, especially in connection with Italian art. Much of the Italian painting of the fourteenth and fifteenth centuries was executed directly on the plastered walls of churches, monasteries and palaces. This method is obviously suitable only in comparatively dry climates; hence its almost exclusive connection with Italy. Even the Venetians found it impracticable in the damp air of their lagoons, and in its place used canvas stretched into wooden frames fastened on the walls. In true fresco, *buon fresco*, as the Italians call it, the colours, moistened with water, are painted on to a damp plaster ground, previously prepared on the wall. As this dries, a chemical process takes place, by which the colours are firmly bound in with the plaster, the painting thus becoming an integral part of the wall itself. As in this true fresco the work must be done while the plaster is still damp, the painter prepares only so much of the wall-surface as he thinks he can paint in one day, at the end of which he scrapes away any plaster that is still uncovered. The next day he lays another expanse adjoining the surface already painted. It is possible in some frescoes, even by means of photographs, to detect these joints in the plaster, and thus to estimate how much the painter was able to accomplish in one day. In Michelangelo's *Adam* on the ceiling of the Sistine Chapel, it is easy to see where the painter left off after each sitting. From its very nature fresco-painting demands broad, rapid treatment and great sureness of hand. Nothing can be altered when once the plaster has dried, unless indeed the artist entirely destroys his work, scrapes away the painted ground and lays a fresh one. Painters who were not sufficiently skilful to finish their work in one sweep, as it were, added afterwards touches *a secco*, when the plaster was dry. These additional touches were added in tempera.

In the Middle Ages, before the introduction of an oil medium, tempera was universally used for altar-pieces and easel pictures, and even afterwards was not entirely discarded. In this method the ordinary medium for mixing and applying the colours was yolk of egg, and it is in this sense that Vasari uses the term tempera. The colours were laid upon prepared panels, and were afterwards varnished. If fresco requires broad, rapid, effective treatment, tempera lends itself to minute delicacy of touch, refinement and finish. The medium being one that dries rapidly, the colours are usually stippled on with fine sable brushes, in a succession of small strokes. Hence a certain dryness of effect and a want of depth, the colours not flowing and blending as in oil-painting. The permanence of the egg medium is one of its great advantages. Many pictures dating from four centuries ago appear as fresh and brilliant as though painted only yesterday.

It was not until the fifteenth century that oil-painting came into general use. For centuries painters, aware of its valuable qualities, had experimented with oil as a medium, but its thickness and clumsiness as compared with other mediums had always seemed to render it unsuitable for fine work. Yet tempera had its drawbacks also, in its very quality of dryness and want of flow. The discovery of an oil medium sufficiently refined to be used in the most delicate painting belongs not to Italy but to the North, and was due to the Flemish painters Hubert and Jan van Eyck.   It is, however, more than astonishing that the first picture which has come down to us in the new medium should display such perfect mastery of handling.   The great altar-piece of the *Adoration of the Lamb* shows no trace of inexperienced or tentative technique.   The colours are warm and transparent, with a depth and gloss unknown to tempera-painting.   It is clear that the difficulties inherent in the use of the new medium had been already overcome. What Van Eyck's discovery actually was remains a puzzle even to this day.   He seems to have produced, by a mixture of certain oils and resinous substances, a medium which dispensed with the use of a final varnish, being medium and varnish in one.   To render this sufficiently quick-drying and colourless was perhaps the most important of the problems he managed to solve.   The Flemish artists painted on carefully prepared panels, overlaid with a white ground.   Their method was to paint in the picture in grisaille with tempera, finishing it with transparent glazes of oil colour.

This northern method was in due course introduced into Italy by Antonello da Messina towards the end of the fifteenth century.   Already Domenico Veneziano, Baldovinetti and Piero della Francesca, in their experiments with various vehicles, had attempted the use of an oil medium.   Veneziano's *Enthroned Madonna* and Piero's *Nativity*, both in the National Gallery, are painted in oil, and the old legend of Castagno's murder of Veneziano for the sake of obtaining this secret points to the interest shown by Italian painters in the great question.   Antonello's innovation worked a revolution in Italian art.   The Italians, and especially the Venetians, used a more solid impasto than did the artists of the North, who painted somewhat thinly. The Venetians also preferred canvas or linen to wooden panels. As a ground canvas offers many advantages over wood. It is more easily obtainable, can be of any size and does not crack. Even its slight roughness of texture may be of use to the painter, who sometimes covers it so thinly with paint that the rough surface below is distinctly visible, just as the Dutch painters on panel would often allow a hint of the brown wood to show through the semi-luminous paint of sky or sea. The life, breadth and freedom displayed in the painting of the sixteenth century had been impossible without the introduction of this new method. Michelangelo alone among his contemporaries refused to work in oil, pronouncing it a method fit only for women, but time has scarcely justified this opinion.

Different as the modern oil picture is from a tempera-painting, and even from the old Flemish method in that the varnish is generally applied over the finished picture, it is by no means easy in every case to determine the medium used in old pictures. Even experts hesitate to pronounce decidedly on some examples, such as Bellini's *Blood of the Redeemer* in the National Gallery, which seem to lie on the borderland between the oil and the older egg medium. The fifteenth century was in this respect a period of transition, the old method being gradually discarded in favour of a new one not as yet perfectly understood. Morelli himself says that in many cases it is impossible to say confidently what particular colours or varnishes the painter has made use of, nor even to decide whether the picture is painted entirely in tempera or finished with glazes of oil. But, generally speaking, there is a sufficiently marked difference between the careful, minute and precise method of a typical tempera picture and the freer, more flowing effect of oil-painting. Compare, for example, in the National Gallery, Filippo Lippi's *Annunciation* and *St. John and Saints* and Crivelli's *Annunciation*, all in tempera, with the pictures by Andrea del Sarto, Titian and Veronese. Here the distinction is marked and offers no question. The early Flemish oil-paintings, on the other hand, are as minute and delicate in execution as anything in tempera, but their greater flow and luminous depth, and the absence of small brush-marks, abundantly illustrate the difference. Even after oil came into universal use as a medium, tempera was used by many artists for the underpainting, in the Flemish manner. Oil-painting indeed may be either transparent or opaque, applied in thin washes or glazes of transparent colour, allowing the underpainting to show through, or directly in thick masses of solid colour, giving a texture that suggests Gandy's ideal of rich cream or cheese.

Every painter has his own manner of actually laying the colours on the ground. Some pictures present a perfectly even surface, others show hills and dales of solid paint. Either manner may be used effectively or the reverse. How exquisite in the fineness of their texture and quality are the little pictures of Terburg, how dull and lifeless the smooth waxen surface of Van der Werff or Denner! What character do the works of Rembrandt and Constable derive from their rough, rugged texture, the irregularities of surface cunningly contrived to catch the light and to cast almost imperceptible shadows! The coarse, unpleasant texture of too many modern pictures is the result, not of deliberate intention, but of an inadequate appreciation of the actual beauties of paint.

Water-colour only came into general use in the nine-teenth century, and is almost exclusively associated with English painting, though French and Dutch artists are now beginning to adopt it, and it was known to Dürer and van Ostade.   It is the most transparent of all medi-ums.   The colours are merely washed on, the paper being left almost white for the high lights, though to-day many painters rely also on body colour.   Owing to this trans-parency and its rapid-drying qualities, water-colour, as we have seen, is peculiarly adapted to catch every passing atmospheric or light effect, the most delicate and subtle nuances of tone, and it is enough to glance at the work of such classical exponents of water-colour as Cozens, Turner, Girtin, Cotman, Varley, David Cox and De Wint to realise to what infinitely various treatment the medium lends itself.

Pastel, now a very fashionable method, is perhaps the least durable of all.   It is as opaque as water-colour is transparent, its most beautiful qualities, as seen in the works of its great exponent, John Russell, being its velvety look, bloom and dull softness.   These are lost by painters who fall into the error of treating pastel as they would oil colour, thus missing the characteristic beauties of both.   From the fact of its dryness, so little medium being mixed with the colours that they remain in powder, pastel pictures are inclined to be sensitive to movement or jar.

In painting, as in all art, good craftsmanship is essential to success.   An artist may be filled with noble ideas and fine inspiration, but if his hands refuse to obey the prompting of the mind, his good intentions can never take beautiful and permanent shape.   His reputation will ultimately depend not more on his natural genius, his artistic sense, than on his sureness of eye and technical skill, his actual power over his materials. These are only to be gained by prolonged and severe training. Some possess these acquired qualities alone, and remain craftsmen to their dying day. Others, more artistically endowed, fail from lack of experience in technical matters, and their power is wasted in even more pitiful fashion. An artist's fame depends ultimately on the permanence of his work, and permanence can only be insured by knowledge, practice and good workmanship. Accident and ill-usage may indeed spoil or destroy the most carefully executed painting. The older a picture, the greater the risks it has run. But time is not the worst enemy to painting. Many a picture dating from the fourteenth or fifteenth century is in better condition to-day than others of a much more recent date. Some of Reynolds's paintings perished almost in the artist's lifetime. Many of Turner's are already practically wrecks. And yet these are but a hundred years old, while innumerable Flemish and Italian pictures of the fifteenth century are in perfect preservation, despite the many vicissitudes of weather, dirt and travel they have endured. It is wonderful how much ill-usage a soundly painted picture can stand, without complete deterioration. Who would believe that Jan van Eyck's portrait of his wife was discovered in the fish market of Bruges, completely concealed by dirt? Michelangelo's unfinished *Entombment* in the National Gallery was rescued from a somewhat similar situation and sold in Rome for a mere song.

Apart, however, from accident, the life of a picture depends on the way it is painted, on the materials used and the care taken to insure their endurance. A painter who uses bad pigments, untried mediums or ill-seasoned panels can scarcely expect his pictures to last. In such matters of craftsmanship the modern world, for all its science, is behind the Middle Ages, when technical skill and excellence of materials were justly insisted on as essential to painting. The long apprenticeship to be served before it was possible to qualify as a master-painter helped to insure a high standard, an apprentice-ship not alone in the actual art of painting, but in the preparation of the materials used, the grinding of the colours, manipulation of the medium and the laying of the ground. The artist thought it no shame to be his own colourman. These preliminaries are seldom under-taken by the painter of our day. There are no guilds to enforce the application of sound materials and work-manship. It is said of Gerard Dou that, when preparing his colours, in order to insure their purity, he made the windows of his studio air-tight to exclude dirt, entered slowly to raise the minimum of dust and waited for it to subside before venturing to take out his palette and brushes. The modern artist buys his pigments and var-nishes ready made, with often the most scanty know-ledge of their chemical properties and probable changes.

Will the paintings of our day, such indeed as from the purely artistic point of view shall survive the verdict of time, endure for centuries as have those of Titian, Correggio and Rubens, or, to go even further back, of Angelico, Roger van der Weyden and the Van Eycks? If permanence be one of the conditions of artistic fame, it would seem that modern painters care far less for reputation than did their predecessors of old. The glory has departed from many of Turner's most brilliant works, because of his carelessness in the preparation of the col-ours he used and his extraordinary mixture of methods. Supreme master as he was of both oil and water-colour, he sometimes used both mediums in the same picture, treating oil in the manner of water-colour. We cannot wonder that his canvases are faded and cracked. Yet who would maintain that Turner was callous to fame, Turner whose will if nothing else proved his ambition to be remembered by posterity?

Other pictures have suffered and even perished because the painters experimented with their materials, using untried pigments and varnishes. The wreck of Leonardo's *Last Supper* is chiefly due to his having painted it on the wall in oil instead of fresco, with the result that even his pupil Lomazzo declared it to be already completely ruined. The colour of his *Mona Lisa* has already considerably faded. Reynolds's works have suffered from the same reckless experimenting. There are comparatively few of his pictures that have not either darkened, faded or cracked. His *Holy Family*, which formerly hung in the National Gallery, has been withdrawn on account of its ruined condition. A wit of the day, whose portrait Sir Joshua had painted with such fugitive pigments that it faded almost immediately, avenged himself for this premature decease in the well-known epigram :

Painting of old was surely well designed
To keep the features of the dead in mind,
But this great rascal has reversed the plan,
And made his picture die before the man.

This deterioration was largely the result of a liberal use of bitumen, that " plague of pictures," so much relied on by painters of that day both in England and France. Many of the pictures of the eighteenth century have suffered from the use of this as of other dangerous pigments. The deep shadows which now seem opaque, black and heavy, were once luminous, reflecting instead of absorbing light. Even comparatively brilliant colours lose their brightness, go in as it were, vivid landscape greens changing to dull indigo or even black, delicate flesh tints to a heavy brown, the whole picture becoming untoned. Whether or not they avail themselves of it, there can be no doubt that, with the advanced knowledge of chemistry that prevails in our day, painters have every means of determining, before using their pigments and mediums, exactly how each will behave, which are permanent, which fugitive, which mutually destructive. The lapse of centuries has proved that it is not safe in oil-painting to correct a mistake or make an alteration by covering it thinly with paint. In time, the under-painting will work through to the surface, and the alter-ation stand revealed. Such corrections or *pentimenti*, as the Italians called them, may be seen in several pictures in the National Gallery, notably in Antonello da Messina's *Salvator Mundi*, where the position of the hand has been altered, and in Gainsborough's *Musidora*, in which a superfluous leg is distinctly visible.

Time, which can thus betray the artist's original in-tention, plays a varying game with pictures, mellowing and maturing some, aging and spoiling others by blackening or fading. Unlike architecture, painting is never beautiful in ruin. Yet the tender hand of time may often bring into harmony colours which, when fresh, perhaps seemed crude and glaring. Where the work-manship is sound, time tones and ripens, however piti-lessly it may operate where it is bad. It is not, however, just to attribute the dusky appearance of all old pictures to the effects of time. No paintings could be blacker in tone than those of Tintoretto in the Scuola di San Rocco at Venice. We know from Vasari that they were so, even when newly painted. To fresco-paintings, indeed, the lapse of years is never kind, often exposed as they are to the effects of damp and changes of temperature.

It is, perhaps, true to say that more pictures have been spoiled by restoration, whether in the form of cleaning or repainting, than from any other preventible cause. Skilful and tactful restoration may indeed give back to a picture something of its first freshness and beauty, but it is often far better to leave well and even ill alone, or at least to do the minimum of doctoring. Where a picture has been repeatedly covered with coat upon coat of dark, heavy varnish, or has been begrimed with the smoke of altar candles or the dirt of the sacristan's broom, much can be done to remove them without injury to the painting. On the other hand, it too often happens that in so doing some of the delicate transparent surface-glazes are carried away, leaving the picture raw and flayed, and where pictures are painted with an oil varnish, in the old Flemish method, cleaning spells certain injury, for the varnish is actually part of the picture. Some of the pictures even in the National Gallery have been thus over-cleaned, greatly to their detriment.

Worse, however, than any over-cleaning is the drastic repainting which many pictures have suffered ; the careful retouching of parts that have been rubbed or cracked is legitimate enough, but the restorer seldom stops here. In some cases he daubs over the picture so completely as to alter its whole appearance. It is very little Laguerre has left us under its disguise of new paint of Mantegna's superb *Triumph of Julius Caesar*, now a ruin at Hampton Court. Such so-called " restoration " is worse than criminal. Unfortunately the picture-restorer is but rarely an artist, and not always a man of taste and sympathy. In many cases in the great galleries the coarse repainting, especially of the eighteenth century, which disfigured so many fine pictures, has been again removed, but enough may still be seen to show how common the practice had become and how pitiful the results.

Lastly, a word may be said as to the framing of pictures. We are gradually breaking loose from the modern tradition of massive gilt frames for all and sundry, a tradition to which the Royal Academy, however, with characteristic conservatism, still clings. The fashion seems to have been initiated in England by Lawrence, who as its President was certain of a following; and gradually the narrow, unobtrusive, but well-designed frames used in the eighteenth century were superseded by a more showy style. To-day the suitable framing of a picture is rightly considered of great importance, as contributing to the decorative effect of the whole. In this we are returning to the practice of the Renaissance, when the frame was often in its own way as beautiful in design as the picture set in it. Without in any way drawing attention from the picture, the exquisite old blue and gold frames in which such pictures as Mantegna's San Zeno Altar-piece and Bellini's Frari *Madonna* are set add immeasurably to the beauty and dignity of the pictures within. Most of the great galleries have now returned to the original manner of framing old Dutch pictures in heavy black or brown frames, just as we see them hanging on the wall in Vermeer and Metzu's interiors. A Dutch genre picture looks out of place in a gilt frame, the quieter setting suiting it far better.

GIOVANNI BELLINI ALTAR-PIECE

Alinari photo] *[Frari, Venice*

INDEX

M

INDEX

CHISWICK PRESS: PRINTED BY CHARLES WHITTINGHAM AND CO.
TOOKS COURT, CHANCERY LANE, LONDON.

CPSIA information can be obtained at www.ICGtesting.com
Printed in the USA
LVOW010222170513

334135LV00005B/789/P

9 781313 377706